Don Carlos, or, An historical relation of the unfortunate life and tragical death of that Prince of Spain, son to Philip the II written in French anno 1672 and newly Englished by H.J. (1676)

Saint-Réal

Don Carlos, or, An historical relation of the unfortunate life and tragical death of that Prince of Spain, son to Philip the II written in French anno 1672 and newly Englished by H.J.
Saint-Réal, M. l'abbé de 1639-1692.
[8], 160 p.
London : Printed by J.G. for Hen. Herringman and Jon Crump, 1676.
Wing / S354
English
Reproduction of the original in the Bodleian Library

Early English Books Online (EEBO) Editions

Imagine holding history in your hands.

Now you can. Digitally preserved and previously accessible only through libraries as Early English Books Online, this rare material is now available in single print editions. Thousands of books written between 1475 and 1700 and ranging from religion to astronomy, medicine to music, can be delivered to your doorstep in individual volumes of high-quality historical reproductions.

We have been compiling these historic treasures for more than 70 years. Long before such a thing as "digital" even existed, ProQuest founder Eugene Power began the noble task of preserving the British Museum's collection on microfilm. He then sought out other rare and endangered titles, providing unparalleled access to these works and collaborating with the world's top academic institutions to make them widely available for the first time. This project furthers that original vision.

These texts have now made the full journey -- from their original printing-press versions available only in rare-book rooms to online library access to new single volumes made possible by the partnership between artifact preservation and modern printing technology. A portion of the proceeds from every book sold supports the libraries and institutions that made this collection possible, and that still work to preserve these invaluable treasures passed down through time.

This is history, traveling through time since the dawn of printing to your own personal library.

Initial Proquest EEBO Print Editions collections include:

Early Literature

This comprehensive collection begins with the famous Elizabethan Era that saw such literary giants as Chaucer, Shakespeare and Marlowe, as well as the introduction of the sonnet. Traveling through Jacobean and Restoration literature, the highlight of this series is the Pollard and Redgrave 1475-1640 selection of the rarest works from the English Renaissance.

Early Documents of World History

This collection combines early English perspectives on world history with documentation of Parliament records, royal decrees and military documents that reveal the delicate balance of Church and State in early English government. For social historians, almanacs and calendars offer insight into daily life of common citizens. This exhaustively complete series presents a thorough picture of history through the English Civil War.

Historical Almanacs

Historically, almanacs served a variety of purposes from the more practical, such as planting and harvesting crops and plotting nautical routes, to predicting the future through the movements of the stars. This collection provides a wide range of consecutive years of "almanacks" and calendars that depict a vast array of everyday life as it was several hundred years ago.

Early History of Astronomy & Space

Humankind has studied the skies for centuries, seeking to find our place in the universe. Some of the most important discoveries in the field of astronomy were made in these texts recorded by ancient stargazers, but almost as impactful were the perspectives of those who considered their discoveries to be heresy. Any independent astronomer will find this an invaluable collection of titles arguing the truth of the cosmic system.

Early History of Industry & Science

Acting as a kind of historical Wall Street, this collection of industry manuals and records explores the thriving industries of construction; textile, especially wool and linen; salt; livestock; and many more.

Early English Wit, Poetry & Satire

The power of literary device was never more in its prime than during this period of history, where a wide array of political and religious satire mocked the status quo and poetry called humankind to transcend the rigors of daily life through love, God or principle. This series comments on historical patterns of the human condition that are still visible today.

Early English Drama & Theatre

This collection needs no introduction, combining the works of some of the greatest canonical writers of all time, including many plays composed for royalty such as Queen Elizabeth I and King Edward VI. In addition, this series includes history and criticism of drama, as well as examinations of technique.

Early History of Travel & Geography

Offering a fascinating view into the perception of the world during the sixteenth and seventeenth centuries, this collection includes accounts of Columbus's discovery of the Americas and encompasses most of the Age of Discovery, during which Europeans and their descendants intensively explored and mapped the world. This series is a wealth of information from some the most groundbreaking explorers.

Early Fables & Fairy Tales

This series includes many translations, some illustrated, of some of the most well-known mythologies of today, including Aesop's Fables and English fairy tales, as well as many Greek, Latin and even Oriental parables and criticism and interpretation on the subject.

Early Documents of Language & Linguistics

The evolution of English and foreign languages is documented in these original texts studying and recording early philology from the study of a variety of languages including Greek, Latin and Chinese, as well as multilingual volumes, to current slang and obscure words. Translations from Latin, Hebrew and Aramaic, grammar treatises and even dictionaries and guides to translation make this collection rich in cultures from around the world.

Early History of the Law

With extensive collections of land tenure and business law "forms" in Great Britain, this is a comprehensive resource for all kinds of early English legal precedents from feudal to constitutional law, Jewish and Jesuit law, laws about public finance to food supply and forestry, and even "immoral conditions." An abundance of law dictionaries, philosophy and history and criticism completes this series.

Early History of Kings, Queens and Royalty

This collection includes debates on the divine right of kings, royal statutes and proclamations, and political ballads and songs as related to a number of English kings and queens, with notable concentrations on foreign rulers King Louis IX and King Louis XIV of France, and King Philip II of Spain. Writings on ancient rulers and royal tradition focus on Scottish and Roman kings, Cleopatra and the Biblical kings Nebuchadnezzar and Solomon.

Early History of Love, Marriage & Sex

Human relationships intrigued and baffled thinkers and writers well before the postmodern age of psychology and self-help. Now readers can access the insights and intricacies of Anglo-Saxon interactions in sex and love, marriage and politics, and the truth that lies somewhere in between action and thought.

Early History of Medicine, Health & Disease

This series includes fascinating studies on the human brain from as early as the 16th century, as well as early studies on the physiological effects of tobacco use. Anatomy texts, medical treatises and wound treatment are also discussed, revealing the exponential development of medical theory and practice over more than two hundred years.

Early History of Logic, Science and Math

The "hard sciences" developed exponentially during the 16th and 17th centuries, both relying upon centuries of tradition and adding to the foundation of modern application, as is evidenced by this extensive collection. This is a rich collection of practical mathematics as applied to business, carpentry and geography as well as explorations of mathematical instruments and arithmetic; logic and logicians such as Aristotle and Socrates; and a number of scientific disciplines from natural history to physics.

Early History of Military, War and Weaponry

Any professional or amateur student of war will thrill at the untold riches in this collection of war theory and practice in the early Western World. The Age of Discovery and Enlightenment was also a time of great political and religious unrest, revealed in accounts of conflicts such as the Wars of the Roses.

Early History of Food

This collection combines the commercial aspects of food handling, preservation and supply to the more specific aspects of canning and preserving, meat carving, brewing beer and even candy-making with fruits and flowers, with a large resource of cookery and recipe books. Not to be forgotten is a "the great eater of Kent," a study in food habits.

Early History of Religion

From the beginning of recorded history we have looked to the heavens for inspiration and guidance. In these early religious documents, sermons, and pamphlets, we see the spiritual impact on the lives of both royalty and the commoner. We also get insights into a clergy that was growing ever more powerful as a political force. This is one of the world's largest collections of religious works of this type, revealing much about our interpretation of the modern church and spirituality.

Early Social Customs

Social customs, human interaction and leisure are the driving force of any culture. These unique and quirky works give us a glimpse of interesting aspects of day-to-day life as it existed in an earlier time. With books on games, sports, traditions, festivals, and hobbies it is one of the most fascinating collections in the series.

The BiblioLife Network

This project was made possible in part by the BiblioLife Network (BLN), a project aimed at addressing some of the huge challenges facing book preservationists around the world. The BLN includes libraries, library networks, archives, subject matter experts, online communities and library service providers. We believe every book ever published should be available as a high-quality print reproduction; printed on-demand anywhere in the world. This insures the ongoing accessibility of the content and helps generate sustainable revenue for the libraries and organizations that work to preserve these important materials.

The following book is in the "public domain" and represents an authentic reproduction of the text as printed by the original publisher. While we have attempted to accurately maintain the integrity of the original work, there are sometimes problems with the original work or the micro-film from which the books were digitized. This can result in minor errors in reproduction. Possible imperfections include missing and blurred pages, poor pictures, markings and other reproduction issues beyond our control. Because this work is culturally important, we have made it available as part of our commitment to protecting, preserving, and promoting the world's literature.

GUIDE TO FOLD-OUTS MAPS and OVERSIZED IMAGES

The book you are reading was digitized from microfilm captured over the past thirty to forty years. Years after the creation of the original microfilm, the book was converted to digital files and made available in an online database.

In an online database, page images do not need to conform to the size restrictions found in a printed book. When converting these images back into a printed bound book, the page sizes are standardized in ways that maintain the detail of the original. For large images, such as fold-out maps, the original page image is split into two or more pages

Guidelines used to determine how to split the page image follows:

• Some images are split vertically; large images require vertical and horizontal splits.
• For horizontal splits, the content is split left to right.
• For vertical splits, the content is split from top to bottom.
• For both vertical and horizontal splits, the image is processed from top left to bottom right.

DON CARLOS:

OR AN

Hiſtorical Relation

OF THE

UNFORTUNATE LIFE

AND

TRAGICAL DEATH

OF THAT

PRINCE of SPAIN,

Son to *Philip* the II.

Written in French Anno 1672, *and newly Engliſhed by* H. J.

LONDON:

Printed by *J.G.* for *Hen. Herringman,* at the Blue Anchor in the Lower Walk of the New Ex-change; and *John Crump,* at the Three Bibles in S.*Pauls* Churchyard. 1676.

TO THE
LADY ELLIS,

Wife to the Right Worshipful

Sir *William Ellis*, Baronet.

Madam,

Eing lately necessitated to pass some days in a place where I had but little Company, and less Diversion, I resolved to spend my Idle Hours in Translating this Relation of the Misfortunes of poor *Don Carlos.*

It was written by a Person of Honour, and one that pretends to have a particular Insight into the *Spanish* History.

Yet a

Yet, leſt his Authority ſhould not ſeem ſufficient in ſome Dubious Paſſages, he backs it with that of the moſt Famous Writers of the laſt Age.

His Deſign (as you may ſee by his own Advertiſement) was chiefly to vindicate the Queen of *Spains* Vertue, from the Aſperſions that had been caſt upon it by ſome Malicious Pens : and mine is no other than to divert you, and by this ſmall Teſtimony of my Affection to aſſure you that I am,

M A D A M,

Your moſt Humble and moſt Obedient Servant,

H. J.

ADVERTISEMENT

OF THE

AUTHOR.

ALL Hiſtorians of the laſt Age, that make mentiꞁn of the Unfortunate Prince of Spain, who is the ſubjeᴄt of this Treatiſe, dꞁ alſo ſpeak of his Love for his Mother in Law ; and as people are alwꞁys apt to put an evil Interpretation upꞁn things of that nature, his Paſſiꞁn hath dꞁne ſome wrꞁng to the Reputation of that Vertuꞁus Queen. The Author of this Bꞁok having found in divers places the Particularities ꞁf their

A 3   Hi-

History, thought himself obliged to communicate them to the Publick, because they justifie the Memory of that Princess, and make it appear, that there was nothing but what was very Innocent on Her side. Though she had done nothing else but discover the Conspiracy, whereof you shall see the recital, she had well deserved to have some care taken of her Glory, because it is certainly true, that without her, the Prince of Navarre had never come to be the greatest King in the world, and (to say something more to his Honour) Grandfather to Lewis the Fourteenth.

This History is taken out of all the Authors, Spanish, French, Italian, and Dutch, which have written

ten of those *Times in which it happened.* *The principal are,* Thuanus, *Monsieur* Aubigné, Brantome, Cabrera, Campana, Adriani, Natalis Comes, Dupleix, Mathieu, Mayerne, Mezerai, le Laboureur sur Castelnau, Strada, Meteren, the History of Don John of Austria, the Elogies of F. Hilarion de Coste, the Spanish Book of the Deeds and Sayings of Philip the second, a Relation of the Death and Obsequies of his Son, &c. *It is likewise collected out of several Pieces pertaining to History, as well Manuscripts as Printed, and amongst the rest cut of a little Book intituled,* Diogenes *, which treats largely of this matter, and a Manuscript written by* Monsieur de Peresese, *expresly*

A 4   up.n

upon that subject. However for the Readers further satisfaction I have set down in the Margin, the most particular and extraordinary places of the principal Authors out of which they were taken.

DON

DON CARLOS:

OR,

An Historical Relation of the Unfortunate Life and Tragical Death of that Prince of Spain, Son to Philip the II.

WHEN the Emperour *Charles* the Fifth resolved to quit the Government of the Empire, and to retire himself into a solitary way of Living ; fearing to leave his Son exposed to the good fortune of *Henry* the Second, of which himself had already felt the Effects, he concluded with that Prince a Truce for the five first years of his Sons Reign. Amongst

A 5   other

other Propofitions for a Peace between the two Crowns, which were
made during this Truce, was propofed the Marriage of *Don Carlos* Prince
of *Spain*, and onely Son of *Philip* the
Second, and *Mary* of *Portugal* his firft
Wife, with *Madam Elizabeth* the eldeft Daughter of *France*. This Princefs was very Young, but wonderfully accomplifhed for a Perfon of her
age. And as this Marriage was re-
folv'd upon with great joy on both
fides, as foon as it was propofed fhe
could not chufe but conceive a very
great Efteem for him that was deftin'd to be her Husband; her young
Heart finding in that occafion a fuit-
able Object to fix it felf upon, did
much pleafe it felf in the thoughts of
it; and fhe did by degrees infenfibly
engage her felf in an Inclination
which (though altogether innocent)
did afterwards prove more trouble-
fom to her Vertue, than ever fhe
thought it would. The Prince of
Spain was no lefs contented than fhe
with

with his hoped for Happiness; and as
all that People said to him concerning *Madam*, gave him a very lovely
Idæa of her Person, he abandon'd
himself with Pleasure to all those
thoughts of Love and Desire which
that *Idæa* inspir'd him withall. The
Princess's Picture, which (according
to the Custom) was sent him by the
King of *France*, finished that Con-
quest in him, which the reputation
of her Beauty had already begun.
Those that brought it, said, it was
extremely like her; and *Don Carlos*
easily believ'd them in a thing he so
much desired might be true. When
he considered this Picture, there was
no way that he would not willingly
have tried to let *Madam* know the
thoughts he had of her. He could
by no means endure that she should
be ignorant of the joy which the
hopes of possessing her fill'd him with.
Sometimes he was even asham'd of
the excess of his good fortune, and
could almost have been contented to

al-

allow himself the time of winning the Princess's heart by his Merits and Services, rather than to obtain her by the common ways; but knowing that to be an impossible thing, he thought he should be well enough satisfied if he could but at least acquaint her with the diversity of his thoughts.

In the mean time the Face of Affairs was wholly changed by a sudden and unexpected breach of the Five Years Truce, the Princes of the House of *Lorrain*, or those that at the Sollicitation of *Paul* the Fourth, brought about this Rupture. The Pope's aim was, by raising Troubles in *Flanders* to free himself from the Duke *d'Alva*, who had the Command of a *Spanish* Army, and had for some time kept him as it were block'd up within the Walls of *Rome*. One part of his Design, which was the diversion of the *Spanish* Arms, succeeded according to his desire; but in *Flanders* he found more Opposition, where the *French* lost two Battels, in which

which the greateſt part of their moſt
Valiant men were either kill'd or taken Priſoners; and (which reduc'd
their Affairs to ſo ill a condition) that
they reſolv'd ſpeedily to buy a Peace
at what price ſoever. This Peace was
the work of the Duke of *Savoy*, General of the *Spaniſh* Army, and of the
Conſtable of *Montmorency* his Priſo-
ner. The Conſtable repreſented to
the Duke, that he could never hope
to find a fairer occaſion of recover-
ing the poſſeſſion of his Eſtates, from
which his Father had been driven by
Francis the Firſt; and the Duke on
his ſide prevailed ſo far with *Philip*
the Second, that the Treaty was concluded a little while after at *Chateau-
Cambreſis*. It is eaſie to judge of the
grief of *Don Carlos* at the breaking of
the Truce, and how great his joy was
when the Negotiation of Peace was
reaſſumed; and yet this Peace which
ſeemingly gave ſuch ſeaſonable
grounds for his hopes was that which
at laſt proved their utter deſtruction.

Du-

During the time of the Negotiation, *Philip* the Second was made a Wi-
dower by the death of *Mary* Queen
of *England*, his second Wife ; and
being obliged by several weighty
Considerations to a third Marriage,
he demanded for himself the Princess
that had before been promised to his
Son.   The *French* would doubtless
much rather have given her to the
Heir of the Crown, who was much of
the same Age with her, than to a
Prince old enough to have been her
Father, and by whom she could have
none but younger Children, and by
confequence incapable of inheriting
the Crown : but (all things considered) he could not handsomly be re-
fused.   Though this news was like
the stroke of a Thunderbolt to poor
Don Carlos, who was told it at first
before a great deal of Company, yet
he was enough Master of himself to
hinder any body from taking notice
of the grief it caused in him ; but the
violence he did himself cost him dear
when

when he was alone. All his thoughts were nothing but the continual inspirations of Love and Rage. But the trouble he was in not permitting him to resolve upon, nor the present state of his Fortune to undertake any thing that might ease his mind, his Despair was insensibly turned into Melancholy, and from thence proceeded that reserved way of living which rendered him so odious to the King his Father, who never once dreaming of the true Cause of his discontent, and judging of his Son by himself, did attribute it to the impatience he thought this young Prince might have of Reigning.

As for *Madam*, though what she felt in her self for *Don Carlos* was rather a disposition to love him, than a true and well established passion, yet the fear she had that there was something more in it than as yet she apprehended, made her have an unspeakable distrust of her self. Till then she had an extreme Curiosity to know

know the effect her Picture had produced upon the Prince; nay and she
had desired sometimes that his heart,
if it were possible, might in that respect enjoy less quiet than her own:
but as soon as she knew the Change
that was happened in their Fortune,
she feared nothing in the World so
much as to be lov'd by him. What
pleasure soever there be to be
thought handsom, she wish'd that
what all people said of her Charms
had been false. In this difference of
thoughts, her Mind not having all the
tranquillity necessary to bring her
handsomly off, in action so hard for a
person in her circumstances, as her
first Arrival at the Court of *Spain*
was, she stopped her journey as long
as she could have the least appearance
of an excuse; and though the Duke
d'Alva had marri'd her in his Masters
name in the Moneth of *June*, she did
not leave *Paris* till the end of *No-
vember*. She staid to see all the fine
Houses that were in her way, and
did

did not come into the Province of *Aquitane* till the Year was ready to expire, as if thofe delays cou'd have done that in her heart that her own Reafon was not capable of doing. When fhe was at the *Pyrenæan* Mountains, Fortune (that fometimes pleafes her felf in beftowing her favours upon thofe that leaft expect them) helped her to one ftop more than ever fhe had hoped for.

Anthony of *Bourbon*, King of *Navar*, was charged with the Conduct of the Princefs into *Spain*, and he was to remit her upon the Frontier into the hands of the Cardinal of *Burgos* and the Duke *de l'Infantado*. This King poffeffed onely the lower *Navar*, becaufe the upper had been ufurped from his Wife's Great Grandfather by the *Spaniards*; but yet, not to prejudice the right he pretended to upon them both, he would not acknowledge the place that at that time feparated his Dominions from thofe of the King of *Spain* for the

true

true *Spanish* Frontier, but he requi-
red a Declaration from the Deputies,
that the delivery he should make of
the Princess in that place should in
no way hurt his Pretensions. The
Declaration was of too great consequence to be accorded without ex-
press Order, and therefore they were
forced to write to *Madrid,* and expect His Majesty's Answer in the
place where they were. *Philip* would
have been glad to have been spared
this trouble by the Court of *France,*
and that this Commission had been
given to somebody else, rather than
to the King of *Navar.* But the Princes of the House of *Guise,* at that time
the new and absolute Masters of all
Affairs, had their particular reasons
for keeping the Princes of the Bloud
(as much as they could) from appro-
ching the Court or the Kings person,
and their design being onely to seek
out fair pretensions so to do, they
were ravish'd to find so plausible an
one, of delivering themselves from
him

him that troubled them moſt. In
ſhort, the King of *Spain* ſaw himſelf oblig'd, either quickly to ſatis-
fie the King of *Navarre's* demand, or
elſe to bring the buſineſs to a Negotiation, to obtain of the Court
of *France* that he might be called
back, and another ſent in his place.
This laſt way ſeem'd to be of an
inſupportable length for a Prince
that was in expectation of the moſt
lovely perſon in the world for his
Wife. Wherefore this great Poli-
tician ſatisfied, for that time, his
Amorous impatience to the prejudice of his Intereſts, and wrote to
his Deputies to grant the King of
Navarre his demand. Preſently after the Queen began her journey to
Madrid, and was met upon the way
by *Don Carlos*, who was accompanied (beſides many other conſiderable
Perſons) by his Couſin *Alexander
Farneſe* the young Prince of *Parma*,
and by *Rui Gomez de Sylva*, Prince of
Eboli, his Governour, and the Kings
great

[12]

* The Father Hilanois of Cofs. Min. in his Elogy of this Queen.

great * Favorite. At the first news the Queen had of the Prince's coming, such opposite Sentiments did raise themselves in her mind, and did agitate her with so much violence, that she fell into a swoon in her Womans arms, and could not be brought to her self till *Don Carlos* was ready to ask leave to salute her. After the first Civilities, these two Illustrious Persons, taken up with the mutual consideration of each other, left off speaking, and the rest of the Company holding their peace out of respect, there was for some time a Silence extraordinary enough in such an occasi-

* *Brantome* in his *Philip* the Second.

on. * *Don Carlos* was not shap'd according to the exactest Rules of Symmetry; but besides the Excellency of his Complexion, and one of the finest Heads in the wo... his Eyes were so full of Fire and Life, and his Mien was so Lofty and Martial, that he could not

with

with reafon be thought any ways
unpleafing. At firft the wonderful
Beauty of the Queen did even dazle
his Eyes; but the confideration of
what he had loft in lofing her quickly changed his admiration into for-
row; and forefeeing what he was
like to fuffer for her, he came by degrees to look upon her with fome
kind of fear. In the mean time the
Duke *de l'Infantado* thought that the
Queen ftaid out of civility to know
when it was *Don Carlos* pleafure to
go, and that the Prince out of refpect
ftaid for the fame reafon. This made
him put the Queen in mind, that it
was time to be going; and by that
means he drew them both out of a
greater perplexity than perhaps he
was aware of. The Prince having
taken his place in the Queens Coach,
never lifted his eyes from off her all
the way; and he had all the conveniency he could defire to confider
her, and undo himfelf. The Queen
foon obferved it, and a fecret Senti-
ment

ment, of which she was not the Mi-
stress, made her find some kind of
Sweetness in seeing the disorder *Don
Carlos* was in. Yet she durst not at
first seem to observe him too exactly,
and he could not look upon her without trembling. But at last their eyes,
after having avoided one anothers
rencounter for some time, not able to
do themselves any further violence,
and meeting one another by chance,
had not the force to withdraw themselves from the Contemplations of so
Tempting Objects. It was by these
faithful Interpreters, that *Don Carlos*
told the Queen all he had to say to
her. He prepared her by a thousand
sad and passionate looks to suffer all
the obstinacy and greatness of his
passion. The Heart of this Prince,
burden'd by its own secret, and pres-
sed with the grief of its misfortune,
could no longer defer to ease it self;
and the Opinions he conceived by
the troubled and discomposed carriage of the Queen, that she was not

ig-

ignorant of his meaning, gave him so
sensible a joy, that it made him forget for some moments both the good
fortune of his Father, and his own
unhappiness. This little satisfaction
gave him a liberty of mind at the
first meeting of the King and Queen,
which otherwise he could not have
hoped for ; but the Princess was so intent upon her melancholy thoughts,
that the presence of her Husband
could not draw her out of them.
When they were arrived at *Madrid*,
and that the King had received her
at her coming out of the Coach, after
the first Ceremonies practised in those
occasions, she set her self to look fixedly upon him, without thinking on
what she did, as if she had observed
whether or no he took notice of the
trouble she was in. *The   * Brantome *in*
King, far enough from *his Discourse of*
suspecting the true cause *this Queen.*
of her disturbance, ask'd her roughly
enough, *Whether she were displeased to
see that his head was already full of*
gray

gray hairs ? Thefe words were taken
for an ill *omen* by thofe that ftood
by, and fome judged from that very
time that the union between two
perfons fo different in that, as well
as upon feveral other accounts, could
never be happy.

The Court of *Spain,* that had hear-
kened to the wonders that were com-
monly reported of the Queens Beauty, as to the ordinary Exaggerations
given to the good qualities of Prin-
ceffes, was infinitely aftonifhed when
it faw that all that had been reported of her came fhort of the truth.

This Princefs was born into the
world with all the Advantages Nature could beftow upon her; and
fhe was then in that flourifhing Age
which is requifite to make a perfect
Beauty. All beautiful perfons do not
touch all forts of Hearts; but the
Queen was equally adored by the
People, and in the Court. As often
as fhe fhewed her felf in publick, fo
often fhe triumphed over the Hearts
of

of all those that saw her. It was so
hard to see her without loving her,
that it is to this day a Tradition in
the Court of *Spain*, * *That*   * Brantome
no wise man would venture *in her Elo-*
to look her long in the Face. *gie.*
In fine, if it be true that Beauty is a
kind of Natural Royalty, one may
say, that never Queen was more pro-
perly Queen than she. It had been
hard that her happy Husband, posses-
sor of so many perfections, should
not have been charmed by them. The
smallest actions and gestures of this
Princess appeared to him extreamly
taking. He found always in her an at-
tracting sweetness, equally different
from the coy severity of the Spanish
Women in publick, & the too extravagant Sallies of their Passion when in
private. Sometimes in making reflection upon these things, he admired his
own happiness, but it was only in
himself; for he did not think it becom-
ing his Grandeur to let so young a
a person know the weakness she was

B   the

the caufe of in him. And if fhe fufpected any thing of it, fhe had quickly
loft that thought, by confidering the
little truft he feemed to put in her, his
fevere carriage towards her, and his re-
gularity to fhut all his careffes within
the bounds of the night, as if he had
been afraid left fhe fhould have feen
him in fome pofture lefs grave than
that in which he was ufually feen by o-
ther People. This way of proceeding,
fo little obliging in appearance, and
fo differing from that agreeable un-
rulinefs of the paffions, that ordinarily accompanies the happy condition
of fatisfied Lovers, did in no wife anfwer the *Idea* the Queen had form'd of
the life that two married People, happy enough to love one another, ought
to lead. So that fhe lookt upon her
Husband as a man of whom fhe poffeffed nothing but the Body, and whofe
mind was wholly filled with Politick
thoughts and ambitious defigns. In
the mean time, fhe was fo extreamly
loved by him, that the enjoyment of
                                    her

her, far from diminishing his passion,
did but augment it : whether it were
that the possession of the object loved, which satisfies so fully the desires
of most Husbands, served only to en-
crease his, by discovering to him every day new hidden Beauties, or that
the secret he made to her of his love
redoubled its violence.

In the mean time Don *Carlos* was
marvellously unquiet to know what
thoughts the Queen had of him. And
though every time she lookt upon
him, he thought he discovered in her
eyes a secret and passionate languish-
ing, which appeared not there at other
times, yet he durst not believe even
what he saw : whatsoever impatience
he had, to have a clearer knowledge in
this point, she being but very seldom
alone, during the publick divertisements that were made in honour of her
Wedding, he was a great while without being able to entertain her in private : but at last, fortune, which plea-
seth her self, in furthering those de-

B 2   signs,

defigns, that can have no other then
unhappy events, offer'd him an occafion of fo doing, when he the leaft ex-
pected it. The King being come into
Spain but a little while before the
Queen, had not as yet paid the laft ho-
nors due to the Body of the Emperour,
who then lay in State fome days journeys from *Madrid*, in the Monaftery
of the *Hieronimites*, where he had ended his days. The Queen was well
pleafed to accompany her Hufband in
this Voyage, to fee a Countrey that
was reported to be the moft beautiful
part in all *Spain*. The Convent of the
Hieronimites of St *Juftus* is fcituate in
a Valley at the entrance of *Extramadu-
ra*, which ftretcheth it felf along the
Banks of the River *Guadiana*, from the
Frontiers of *Caftilia* to that of *Portugal*.

This Valley is encompaffed with
hills of an extraordinary height, the
leaft fruitful places of which are covered with thofe eternally-green Trees,
which are not to be found but in thofe
hot

hot Countreys. A thousand little
Brooks, that have their Springs among
these Woods, after many curious tur-
nings and windings cast themselves into a River that crosses the plain ; & the
Soile that is made fertile by this great
quantity of running water, hath always brought forth an infinite number
of *Orange*-Trees, *Lemon*-Trees, and o-
ther such like plants that grow under
this happy Climate. These Brooks in
the hottest days of Summer do maintain in the shady walks of this Desart,
a coolness, which by all the Artifice of
Man cannot be produced in another
place, and the Greens which always
grow upon their Banks have so lively a
lustre, that the pencil of the skilfulest
Painter could never compose one so
beautiful. The Court being arrived
unto this solitude, which *Charles* the
Fifth had rendred so famous by his re-
treat, the King after having perfor-
med the first duties of Piety, would
needs see a young Religious Man that
his Father had much loved; and a-

B 3   mong

among other things he was curious to
know the original of this Friendſhip:
he was told, That the Emperour going
one morning, when it came to his turn,
to wake the other Religious, found
this young Man, who was then a Novice buried in ſo profound a ſleep, that
he had much ado to make him riſe; that
the Novice at laſt getting up with
much diſcontent, and at beſt not half a-
wake, could not keep himſelf from ſay-
ing to him, *That he might well enough be
contented to have troubled the quiet of the
World, ſo long as he had lived in it, without coming to diſturb the repoſe of thoſe
that had forſaken it*; and that this an-
ſwer had ſo taken the Emperour, that
he had teſtified a particular inclination
to him ever after. After ſome other diſ-
courſes, all the Company ſeparated
themſelvs to take a walk in this agreeable Wilderneſs, ſo that the Queen, who
was wearied with the journey, was
left almoſt alone with Don *Carlos*. And
as thoſe that ſtayed with them were
not of a quality to intereſt themſelves

in

in their converſation; Don *Carlos* ra-
viſhed to find ſuch an opportunity,
propoſed to her to go and reſt her ſelf
in a little Wood of *Orange*-trees that
was behind the Appartment of the Emperour; thither they went, and the
Prince who was afraid of being inter-
rupted, preſently began the diſcourſe
with ſuch a liberty as made the Queen
loſe the ſuſpicion ſhe had of his deſign.
At firſt he conjured her not to diſquiet
her ſelf for the things he had to ſay to
her, & to believe that he would never
give her any other trouble than that of
hearing him. Afterwards he beſeeched
her to remember the time, when they
were deſtined from each other, and to
conſider what impreſſion ſo charming
a hope muſt needs have made upon his
heart. *You may eaſily believe, Madam*
(continued he) *that the ſight of you, hath
not defaced this impreſſion; and I feel but
too well, that it will never be defaced in me.*
The Queen at preſent could not keep
her ſelf from taking pleaſure to ſee a
man have ſo paſſionate ſentiments for

B 4   her,

her, & such as no body ever yet durst
testifie to her. But afterwards making
reflection on Don *Carlos*, she comprehended so well their force, & they gave
her so sad an *Idea* of the state of that
Prince's mind, that they made her conceive a great deal of pitty for him. She
confessed to him, *That the esteem she had,
heretofore had for his person, at the time
she was designed to be his Wife, did not permit her to see his suffering without grief,
nor to deny him those consolations which
she could give him without offending her
duty.* The Prince answered her, *That he
pretended to no other consolation then that
of seeing her, and speaking to her:* But the
Queen, who perhaps was afraid of say
ing more then she had a mind to, rose up
at these words, and walking towards
the Prince of *Parma* and *Rui Gomez,*
whom she saw coming towards her, she
only told Don *Carlos, That if he were
wise, and lov'd her truly, far from seeking
her company, he would do what he could to
avoid it.* Don *Carlos* was extreamly satisfied with the Declaration he had
made

made to her of his paffion, and his carriage afterward was as free, as before it feem'd to be conftrain'd. The Queen was one of the firft that took notice of this change: and, as there is no form under which Love may not be difguifed to infinuate it felf into a heart, no not fo much as that of reafon and vertue it felf, fhe thought her felf oblig'd both out of prudence and generofity, to keep fecret the paffion of this Prince. In this thought fhe could not hinder her felf from letting him know, that fhe lookt upon the change of his humor as an effect of his difcretion. Don *Carlos*, the firft time he could find an opportunity of fpeaking to her in private, after the return of the Court to *Madrid*, took the liberty to put her in mind of it; and he affured her, with a great deal of pleafure, that there was no fort of humour, nor manner of life fo contrary to his natural inclination, but his paffion could make him undertake for her fake. After

this,

this, they made one another Confidents of as many particularities of their lives as were fit to be related. Don *Carlos* told the Queen all that had paſſed in his heart and mind, ever ſince the firſt time he had heard her ſpoken of. And ſhe (when he had done ſpeaking) made him the Hiſtory of her Infancy, with a thouſand little circumſtances, which was as agreeable to his intention, as they would have ſeemed tedious to an indifferent perſon. Onely when ſhe came to that part of her Diſcourſe that touch'd the reſolution of their Marriage, ſhe did not enlarge her ſelf upon the Sentiments ſhe had had on that occaſion, with ſo much liberty as the Prince had done upon his; but the violence he ſaw ſhe did her ſelf to hide them, told him more than ſhe concealed. In ſuch pleaſing Entertainments it was that theſe two illuſtrious perſons ſpent the time they could have to be together; when fortune, already weary of favouring

ſo

ſo innocent a commerce, ingaged Don *Carlos* in an adventure, that was the foundation of all his misfortunes.

Of all the Ladies, in whom the Queens beauty cauſed envy and jealouſie, there was none that had greater reaſon to hate her upon that account, then the Princeſs of *Eboli* ; in wit and beauty ſhe ſurpaſſed all the Court, and for this reaſon, as well as becauſe of the great favour her Husband was in with the King, ſhe held the firſt rank among the Ladies. She had an equal Love for magnificence and pleaſure, and, as ſhe thought, nothing capable of reſiſting the charmes of her perſon and wit, ſhe had at firſt form'd a deſign upon the Kings heart : but the Queens beauty having rendred her project fruitleſs, ſhe attempted to make Don *Carlos* in Love with her, not thinking to find in the heart of the Son, the ſame obſtacle that had hindred her ſucceſs with the Father. *Rui Gomez,* in quality of the Princes Governor, was lodged in the ſame Apartment with him; the

the Princess of *Eboli* his Wife, besides
the conveniency of seeing Don *Carlos*,
had often occasion of obliging him, in
reconciling him with her Husband,
with whom he had some little Quar-
rels every day. Don *Carlos* who was
very generous, & who saw with what
zeal she employed her self for him, was
not wanting in gratitude to her for it,
and lived very civilly with her.

These favourable dispositions gi-
ving the Princess good hopes concerning her enterprize, she quickly found
out the means to bring him to the
point she desired. The admiration he
had for the Queen, caused in him a
certain contempt of all other Women. Besides it is well known, that
most young people of that quality
love naturally to divert themselves
to the cost of others, and the flattery
of those that praise them, accustoms
them to those sorts of disobliging jests,
instead of reproving them for it.
Don *Carlos*, who was not exempt
from all the faults of his Age and quality,

lity, and the Prince of *Parma*, yet
younger, and more hot headed then
he, having one day played one of
their ordinary tricks to some women
of the first Quality, who complained
of them, the Princess of *Eboli* had
much ado to obtain of *Rui Gomez*
not to speak of it to the King. That
very night this Woman being alone
in her Closet with Don *Carlos*, she
began to reproach him with the little consideration he had for the Ladies, and after having made him a
thousand Railleries upon that Subject, she concluded, that the friendship she had for him must needs be
very strong, to make her pardon those
kind of things. The Prince who per-
ceiv'd not her design, and who was
oblig'd in gratitude to profess much
affection to her, answered her, laughing, *That she had more reason to employ
her self for him, than perhaps she thought;
because, the little considerations he had
had for all other Women, came from
the Monopoly she had made of all the*
esteem

esteem he *was capable of for that Sex.*
The Princess charmed with those
words, which she took for a declaration of Love, answer'd him in a
manner that opened his Eyes, and
made him perceive his good fortune;
At first he was of the mind to make
use of it, and, it seemed to him, that
never infidelity was more excusable
than that he was going to commit.

This Princess was of those Women, who, without having all their
Features exactly proportioned, have
something that touches more then
the most regular beauties. But,
how dangerous soever she were, Don-
Carlos was yet full of the passion he
had for the Queen, his imagination
represented her to him at that instant,
with those graces and that sweetness,
that made all other Beauties appear
rude and insipid in comparison of hers;
and, the force of this *Idea* made him
all on a sudden look upon the Princess with a disdain, which she had no
reason to expect from him. Yet he
answer'd

answer'd her Compliment in the moft
obliging manner he could, without
fatisfiying her defire: but, fhe faw
well enough that he pretended an
affection which really he had not. A
Woman, that hath feen her felf in
this condition, never forgets it, and
remembers it with rage, if fhe hath
not caufe to remember it with pleafure. We fhall fee the effects this rage
produced in the heart of the Princefs
of *Eboli*; in the mean time, Love,
that had pitty of her Adventure,
brought a new Perfonage upon the
Stage of this Court, to repair the
fault of Don *Carlos*.

It was Don *John* of *Auftria*, Natural Son of *Charles* the Fifth, that
the King took about that time out of
the hands of a *Spanifh* Nobleman,
who had brought him up as his own
Son; and though this young Prince
had always thought himfelf to be
fo, he was as fierce and as ambitious
as if he had known his true birth.
When this *Spaniard* who paffed for
his

his, Father, came to caſt himſelf at his feet, before he preſented him to the King, Don *John* lookt upon him in that poſture with as much tranqui-lity, as if he had a long while ex-pected this change. Seeing nothing in the New Rank he was entred into above his courage, he was not at all dazled with it, and all the Court ſaw with admiration the Son of Don *Lewis Quiſciada* accuſtome himſelf in leſs then half an hours time to act the Son of an Emperor.

This new Prince not being of an humour to make uſe of all precautions neceſſary to defend his heart againſt the charmes of the Queen, fell in Love with her as ſoon as he ſaw her. And whether it were that his paſſion flatter'd his vanity, or that he hoped to make it ſerve to the eſtabliſhment of his fortune, when he perceived it, he made no attempt to cure himſelf of it; and as he was naturally a diſ-ſembler, it was eaſie for him to hide the aſſiduity he manifeſted about the

Queens

Queens Perſon, under the pretext of the neceſſity of his appearance at Court. His overcarefulneſs ſoon diſpleaſed Don *Carlos*; and though this Princeſs would have perſwaded him that ſhe was glad of that obſtacle, to hinder the freedom of their converſation, that ſo ſhe might be leſs expoſed to ſuffer the expreſſions of his Love, yet ſhe conceived an averſion for Don *John*, of which ſhe would not examine the reaſon.

There is no rencounter in the life of Man where diſſimulation is of ſo great uſe, as in love, nor any in which it is harder to diſſemble. The Prince could not always be ſo abſolutely Maſter of his paſſion, when the preſence of Don *John* was troubleſome to him, as that this latter did not at length perceive ſomething thereof; And as there is nothing ſo penetrating as the eyes of a Rival, he had quickly perceived the reaſon of it. This knowledge gave him an extreame curioſity, to know, whether the

the Prince's paſſion were known to
the perſon that cauſed it, and whether
ſhe anſwered it or no. To be the better
inform'd of this, he reſolved to
counterfeit being in Love with a
French woman that waited upon
the Queen, who was handſom e-
nough to render this counterfeit
probable, and who appeared to be
more in her favour then any of her
other women. He ſpared nothing of
all he could imploy to corrupt her;
but it was impoſſible he could draw
from her the ſecret of her Miſtreſs,
becauſe ſhe knew it not ; for, the
Queen, far from acquainting any one
body elſe with it, would have been
glad, if ſhe could, to have hid it from
her ſelf. He took pretence of talking
to this Lady, that ſo he might leave
Don *Carlos* alone with the Queen,
and he became inſenſibly as com-
mode as till then he had been
troubleſome. He thought, that if
they were of intelligence with each
other, he ſhould know nothing of it,
by

by interesting himself in their con-
versations, because they would then
take heed of him, and that his affiduity would but make them hate him
the worse, and keep him the more
out of their privacy, into which he
desired passionately to be admitted.
The Queen appeared so reserved,
that he despaired of entring into hers:
He attempted then to get that of the
Prince, whose free and ingenuous
nature promised him a greater facili-
ty; in this design he changed wholly
his carriage towards him; He used no
more that familiarity which the quality of an Uncle gave him, and he became the most respectful of his Courtiers. He managed so dexterously
the occasions of making people take
notice of Don *Carlos*'s good qualities, that this Prince, who suspected
not his esteem of flattery, because he
knew that he deserv'd it, came by
degrees to think that his Uncle loved him. Don *Carlos* did in the end,
even put a great deal of confidence in
him,

him, but as that of a truly generous
Man, and who loves really, never ex-
tends it felf to the fecret of his love
when he is well ufed: the Prince at
length intrufted all things to his Un-
cles knowledge, befides that one he
defired to know.

Don *John* growing defperate, with
not being able to difcover any thing,
refolved to take counfel of fome body that had more experience than
himfelf in thofe matters. As he was
the handfomeft and beft proportion'd
Prince in Europe, he had at firft
mightily pleafed the Princefs of *Eboli*, who knew not that the Queen
was to be fatal to all her defigns;
Yet, fhe did not wholly fpoile this
laft, as fhe had done the others. Don
John was one of thofe happy com-
plexions, that are never fenfible to
beauty, but in view of the pleafures
it can give; and that of the Princefs
of *Eboli* promifing much, touched at
leaft his fenfes, if it did not reach his
heart, as the Queens had done. On
the

the other fide, he confider'd the Princefs as a perfon whofe Counfels might
ferve him very confiderably, in a
Court, where all things were new to
him. He prevented by his officioufnefs the teftimonies of good will
which fhe fought to give him; and
appeared fo tranfported with joy at
the firft Marks he faw of it in her,
that fhe well judged he would anfwer
to greater with much ardour. So
that they had foon eftablifhed a Commerce, by fo much the more agreeable, as their hearts were not enough
concerned in it to trouble their pleafures by jealoufies, and thofe other
too delicate fcrupulofities, that great
paffions ufe to infpire.

Don *John* living in this manner
with the Princefs of *Eboli*, refolved
fully to acquaint her with all he knew
concerning the Love of Don *Carlos*.
It is eafie to judge of the joy fhe had
at the hearing of this news: fhe was
fo taken up with it, that fhe made no
reflection upon the intereft Don *John*
took

took in the Queens heart: Only she
counselled him, continually to observe all things, because how circum-
spect soever one be , it is impossible
not to forget ones self sometimes,
when one is truly in love. And as
she examined not the interest he
seem'd to take in this matter, so he
was not too curious in searching out
the reason of that zeal, with which
she promised him to employ her self
in it. He thought, without deeper
examination, that it was an effect of
the complaisance she had for him, and
of the curiosity ordinary to those of
her Sex. It is probable, that two so
clear-sighted persons would soon have
discovered, what they had so much
interest to know, if it had not been
for an accident which broke all their
measures, in absenting Don *Carlos*
from the Court, and which cannot
well be understood, without following the Story to its first source.

* Mr. de Thou;   * Among the Reports
Axbigné Etr.   that had run about in the
                                        world

world concerning the Emperours retirement ; the moſt ſtrange of all was, that the continual Negotiations he had had with the Proteſtants of *Germany*, had bred in him ſome inclinations for their Opinions, and that he had hid himſelf in that ſolitude, only to have the greater liberty of ending his dayes in thoſe exerciſes of Piety, that were moſt conformable to his ſecret diſpoſition. It was ſaid, he could not pardon himſelf the ill treatment he had made to thoſe Princes of that Party, that the chance of War had brought into his power. Their vertue, which in the midſt of their misfortune ſhamed his proſperity, had bred in him by degrees ſome ſort af eſteem for their Opinions. He durſt not any longer condemn a Religion, to which ſo many great Perſons made it their glory, to ſacrifice all that men can have moſt precious in the World. This eſteem appeared by the choice he made of perſons, ſtrongly ſuſpe-
ᴄᵗed

ćted of Herefie, for his fpiritual con-
dućt, as of the Doćtor *Cacalla* his
ordinary Preacher; of the Arch-
bifhop of *Toledo*, and above all, of
Conftantine Pontius Bifhop of *Droffa*,
and the Direćtor of his Confcience,
It hath been known fince, that the
Cell where he died at St. *Juftus*,
was filled on all fides with little Papers, written with his own hand,
concerning Juftification and Free
Grace, which was not very far from
the Doćtrine of the Innovators. But
nothing confirmed this opinion fo
much as his Will, there was almoft
no pious Legacies in it, nor any foundations for Prayers for his Soul;
and it was made in a manner fo different from thofe of all zealous Catholicks, that the Inquifition of *Spain*
thought it had right to take notice
of it, yet it durft not make any noife
before the Kings arrival. But this
Prince having fignalized his entry
into that Country, by the exem-
plary punifhment of all that were
ad-

adherents to the new opinion; the
Inquisition growing bolder by his
example, attacked first the Arch-
bishop of *Toledo*, afterwards the Emperours ordinary Preacher, and last
of all *Constantine Pontius*. The King
having suffered them to be imprison-
ed all three, the people look't upon
his patience as a Master-piece of his
zeal for the true Religion; but all
the rest of *Europe* saw with horrour
the Confessor of the Emperour
Charles (in whose arms that Prince
expired, and who had, as it were, received into his Bosome his great
Soul) delivered to the most cruel and
most shameful of all punishments, and
that too by the hands of the King
his Son. In effect, the Inquisition
thinking fit in the prosecution of their
Process, to accuse these three persons
of having an hand in making the
Emperours Will, had the boldness
to condemn them to be burnt with
the Will. The King awaken'd himself at this Sentence as at a clap of

Thun-

Thunder : At firſt the jealouſie he had of his Father's glory, made him find ſome pleaſure in ſeeing his memory expoſed to this affront ; but afterwards having conſidered the conſequences of this attempt, he hinder'd its effect by the moſt gentle and ſecret wayes he could chuſe, thereby to ſave the honour of the holy Office, and make no breach upon the Authority of this Tribunal. As for Don *Carlos*, at the firſt news he received of this buſineſs, he talk'd o it onely as matter fit for raillery ; but ſeeing that the Inquiſition continued in good earneſt its purſuit, he conceived an indignation proportionable to what he owed to the memory of the Emperour. To comprehend the reaſon of the particular intereſt he took in that buſineſs, we muſt know, that this great Perſonage, who, amongſt other heroick qualities, did ſoveraignly poſſeſs that of underſtanding himſelf in men, had conceived extraordinary hopes of his

Grand-

Grandſon. When he retired himſelf
into *Spain,* he would needs have
him along with him: And it was
in that excellent School of Wiſdom
and Magnanimity, that *Don Carlos*
had confirmed himſelf in his natural
love for glory, and for all Princely
vertues. The deſire he had to an-
ſwer worthily the pains of ſo illuſtrious a Preceptor, had in ſome ſort
ripen'd his Wit before the time, and
made it bring forth fruits, that were
not to be hoped for in ſo early a ſea-
ſon. The Emperour knew how to
manage the fiery and violent nature
of the Prince with ſo much artifice
and dexterity, that he had viſibly mo-
derated it in a ſhort time. But it being to be feared, leaſt this great ardour
of mind ſhould incline him to evil
courſes, if he had endeavoured utterly to have ſuppreſſed it, he gave it
all the liberty neceſſary, by encou-
raging him in the purſuit of glory,
of which one may ſay, That this
wiſe Governor abandon'd all the

Beauties

Beauties to the violence of his Pupil's defires. It is eafie to imagine,
that this education had imprinted in
Don Carlos an extraordinary refpect
for the Emperour his Grandfather,
and that the endeavouring to blot
the memory of that illuftrious Deceafed, was an offence to him in the
moft fenfible part of his Soul. *Don
John* and the Prince of *Parma*, interreffed in this glorious memory as well
as he, were not lefs provoked with
the affront. They blamed all three
the King's weaknefs, who did not
refift this infolence with all the violence they could have wifh'd, and
they conceived for him a contempt,
that never ended but with their
lives. And as they were yet too
young to comprehend, that the moft
abfolute Kings have no rights fo facred in the minds of their people, as
thofe that are taken from the pretence of Religion, they fpake publickly of the attempt of the Inquifition with as great tranfports of paffion

on, as people of their quality were capable of having, upon fo juftifiable a fubject; nay, and they went fo far as to threaten, that they would utterly deftroy the holy Office, and all its fupports. The people, who learn'd thefe paffages no otherwife, then as the Inquifitors, or thofe who were employ'd by them, were pleafed to relate them, did teftifie, how extremely they refented fuch proceedings. The King forefaw at the very firft, the ill confequences that might follow unto the Princes from their indignation, but knowing that they had fo far forgot themfelves, as to blame fome of his own actions, he would not fpeak to them of it himfelf, for fear of drawing upon him fome difrefpectful anfwer. *Rui Gomez*, whom he charged with this Commiffion, acquitted himfelf of it with all the earneftnefs, that the importance of the matter feem'd to require. *Don John* and the Prince of *Parma*, who had naturally more the

C 3   maftery

maſtery of themſelves then Don
Carlos, rendred themſelves to his rea-
ſons; and Ambition being their pre-
dominant paſſion, they had all the
ſorrow imaginable, to have put ſo
conſiderable an obſticle to their fortune, as the hatred of the Inquiſitors, which by this means they had
brought upon themſelves, and by
conſequence that of the People.
The Prince on the contrary, whoſe
nature was .to be the more irritated
by oppoſition, could never be brought
to confeſs that he was in the wrong.
In the mean time, the Doctor *Cacalla* was burnt alive, with an Effi-
gics that repreſented *Conſtantine Por-
nius*, who was dead ſome dayes before in the Priſon. The King was forced to ſuffer this Execution, that ſo
he might oblige the holy Office to
ſuffer the Archbiſhop of *Toledo* to ap-
peal to *Rome*, and that the Emperour's
Will might be no more ſpoken of.

This accommodation of affairs appeaſed Don *Carlos*, but it did by no
means

[47]

means pleafe the Inquifitors; and that being a fort of people incapable of pardoning, they raifed fo great murmurings among the people, that what care foever the King could take, there was no way of making the noife ceafe, but by abfenting the Prince from the Court for fome time.

Alcala was then in its greateft luftre, and all the confiderable perfons that went into *Spain*, fail'd not to vifit fo famous an Univerfity. The King pretended, that the Princes had the fame curiofity; and his pretence to haften their Voyage the more, was, that the Prince of *Parma* was fhortly to leave them, and to go under the conduct of the Count of *Egmont* into *Flanders*, where he was to be married. When Don *Carlos* knew this refolution, and that now he muft neceffarily leave the Queen, he began to fee the precipice into which he had thrown himfelf, and the intereft of his love forced from his mind a repentance of

C 4   his

his paſt carriage, which was more
than the intereſt of his ſafety and
greatneſs could ever have done. The
King, who could by no means endure
to be ſeparated from *Rui Gomez*,
obliged the Count of *Egmont* to take
this Favourites place about the
Princes during the Voyage of *Alcala*.
This Count was one of the moſt
accompliſhed Captains of his age,
and was covered with the glory he
had gotten in the laſt War at the
Battels of St. *Quintin* and *Gravelin*,
and of ſo many great men that had
been formed in *Charles* the Fifth's
School, no one had ever had a greater ſhare then he in the eſteem of that
Emperour. The Dutcheſs of *Parma*
well foreſaw the ſtorm, that ſince
that time was raiſed in the Provinces,
which the King her Brother had in-
truſted her with, and ſhe judged it
convenient to repreſent to him the
inconveniences that were to be feared
from thoſe Novelties he had a mind
to introduce. This Commiſſion demanded

manded a man of the quality and pro-
feſſion of the Count of *Egmont*, and
one accuſtomed to ſpeak to Princes
with that noble liberty, which is ſo
uſeful to them, and of which ſo few
of thoſe about them are capable.
Don *Carlos*, who naturally loved all
extraordinary men, engaged the
Count to entertain him, as they rode
along, with a deſcription of the laſt
Battel, in which he had commanded.
The Count, who was charmed with
his curioſity, ſatisfi'd it fully; and
Don *Carlos* made appear an extreme
impatiency of ſeeing himſelf in a condition to do ſomething like that he
heard related; he aſſured the Count
of *Egmont*, that if ever the troubles
in *Flanders* came to break out in an
open War, as the Governeſs ſeem'd
to apprehend they would, nothing
ſhould hinder him from coming into
thoſe Provinces, there to learn under him his Apprentiſhip of War.

The Voyage of the Princes was
not long, the Town of *Alcala* pre-

C 5   ſented

sented Don *Carlos*, with a Horse of
great price; but as furious as he was
handsome. The Prince having desired to see him mounted, was ill satisfied with all those that rode him,
and would needs try how he could
ride him himself: The Horse, whose
mouth was already very much heat-
ed, as soon as the Prince began to
prick him, took a fright, and ran a-
way with him with so much violence, that Don *Carlos* thought it his
best way to throw himself off; but
he did it so unfortunately, that he
was left for dead upon the place;
and though he came to himself some
hours after, yet when the Chirur-
geons had examin'd the wound he
had received in his head, they all
despaired of his life. In this extremity, he sent the Marquess of *Posa*, his
Favourite, to carry his last Adieu to
the Queen. The Princess of *Eboli*
went to him, at the first report she
heard of this accident, to see after
what manner he would receive her.
The

The diffimulation of the Queen, who
was not prepared for fo rude a trial,
abandon'd her at this news; and
though her mouth, accuftom'd to be
filent, did not permit her grief to declare it felf by complaints, her fi-
lence, and the diforder fhe was in,
difcover'd more of her thoughts, then
all the words in the world could
have done. Yet how great foever her
affliction feem'd to be, there had
been always fo much friendfhip feen
between her and Don *Carlos*, that no
body was furprifed therewith. But
the Princefs of *Eboli*, that was a great
proficient in the myfterious Sciences
of Love, could not comprehend, how
fo violent a defpair in the Queen,
fhould be nothing but an effect of
friendfhip. In the mean time the people, infpir'd by the Inquifitors, did
not feem to difcover any great for-
row for this misfortune, but look'd
upon it as a manifeft punifhment of
God upon Don *Carlos* for his impie-
ty. The Queen, who thought fhe had
now

now nothing more to housewife,
could not refuse her self the sad consolation of letting the Prince know,
the pitiful condition in which he left
her. She wrote to him all that love
and dispair can suggest most tender
and most affecting ; and she made
the Marquess of *Posa* go back to
him, with order presently to bring
back her Letter, in case he should not
arrive at *Alcala* till after the death of
Don *Carlos.*

The joy with which the Princes
Soul was filled at the receit of this
Letter was so great, that it restored
him his life. As soon as he was out
of danger, the King made him be
brought back to *Madrid*, thinking
that the annimosity of the people
would in part be appeased by this
cruel adventure. The first time the
Queen saw *Don Carlos*, she ask'd him
for her Letter ; but how earnest soever she were to have it back, the
Prince, to whom this testimony of
her affection was dearer, then the

life

[53]

life of it had rendred him, perfifted always in his refolution to keep it, not thinking that this Letter was once more to decide his deftiny. At his return, he found the Princefs great with child, and her greatnefs did provoke his jealoufie to a degree, that made him make fo odd and unreasonable complaints to her, that any body but fhe would have thought that he had loft his wits. Whilft his Cure was finifhing, fhe lay in, of the Illuftrious Arch-Dutches of *Flanders*, who was afterwards Heirefs of her Beauty and Wit, as well as of her Name. A little while after fhe fell dangeroufly fick of the Small Pox; but the prayers of the people for her were fo effectual, that fhe recovered, not only with a greater degree of health, but alfo * much more beautiful then before. Don *Carlos* had hardly had the time to teftifie his joy to her for her recovery, when fhe

* *Brantome* in his Difcourfes upon this Queen.

she was forced to go to *Bayonne*, whither the Court of *France* was come to meet her, and where the charms of her conversation, and her prudent and modest carriage did not cause less admiration of her in peoples minds, then her beauty caused disturbance in their hearts. Don *Carlos* saw with all the discontent imaginable these divers hinderances, which Fortune raised up one after another to interrupt his commerce with the Queen, when this last Voyage, after which he thought he should have nothing more to fear, drew upon them an affair, which imbitter'd the sweetness of their life by some obstacles, that never had an end.

* *Jeanne de Albret* Queen of *Navarre*, and Widdow of the late King *Anthony*, had a pretty while before this time declared her self of the New Religion; and she was a Princess that govern'd her Subjects with a Piety,

* Mr. *de Tou.*

that

that might well be an example to
all her Sect; and with a Justice,
whose equall perhaps had never been
seen in the Court of any King. Her
Son, whom she brought up in the
same belief, was look'd upon from
that very time by the Religionaries
of *France* as their Protector. The
Spaniards seeing that the pretensions
of that House upon the upper *Navarre*, fell into the hands of this
Child, brought up in an hereditary
hatred against them, that was sharp-
ned by the difference of their Religion, and upheld by a party so re-
doutable, as was that of the *Hugonots* at that time, to deliver themselves from all these fears, resolved
forcibly to make away this young
Prince, with the Queen his Mother &
the Princess his Sister, out of the heart
of their Dominions, and to carry them
into *Spain*, & put them into the hands
of the *Inquisition*. The chief of the
Catholick party in *France*, being of
intelligence with the Duke *D'Al-
                                        va*,

va, to deprive the *Huganots* of so considerable a support, as was that of the House of *Navarre*, engaged themselves with joy to contribute whatsoever depended on them, for the happy success of this enterprise. An infamous Villain called Captain *Dominick*, born in the Countrey of *Bearn*, was charged with the execution of the business, by reason of the perfect knowledge he had of the Countrey. Part of the Troops that waited then at *Barcellona* for a favourable wind to pass iuto *Barbary*, were appointed to advance themselves as far as *Terragona*. From this Town it was easie secretly to lead a considerable Body of Horse through the Mountains, and so to surprise the Queen and her Children at *Pau* in *Bearn*, where they made their residence, and where they had almost no other Guard then the hearts of their Subjects. But though their design were wonderfully well laid, the great destiny of the young Prince
rendred

rendred it vain : It preferved him
to be one day the reftorer of *France*
to its ancient fplendor, and the ter-
rour of the *Spaniards*. A little while
before the voyage of *Bayonne*, Captain *Dominick*, affifted by fome
Governors of the *French* Frontier,
that depended upon thofe who made
him act, had difpofed all things neceffary upon the places appointed
for his attempt. After that he was
gone into *Spain*, where he went to
receive the Orders of the Duke
D'. *Alva*, for the advancement of the
Troops deftin'd for its execution.
The Duke, who was then at *Alva*,
after fome conference with him, fent
him back to the King, who held the
States of the Kingdom at *Mouzon*.
The Captain fell dangeroufly fick in
going thither, and was forc't to ftay
at *Madrid*, where he was neceffarily
to pafs. During his illnefs, he was
affifted in all things by a French man
a fervant to the Queen, and who was
his Country-man ; Not knowing how
to

to teſtifie his gratitude, he chanced one day to ſay to him, *That his life was of greater importance then perhaps he thought, and that the care which was taken of him ſhould be one day magnificently rewarded.* Theſe words were pronounced after a manner that might make one judge, they had ſome extraordinary foundation, and they cauſed in his Friend the curioſity of penetrating the Myſtery they ſeemed to contain. The Captain could refuſe nothing to a Man, to whom he thought he owed his life : And, whether it were that the fear of death had inſpired him with ſome repentance of his crime, or that the Diſeaſe had diſturb'd his brain, he pay'd with this ſecret the ſevices he had received. This Friend told it the ſame day to the Queen his Miſtreſs, who was then at *Madrid*, and who lived in a ſtrait friendſhip with the Queen of *Navarre*.

At the recital of this horrible Plot ſhe could not withhold her tears; and

and whilft the Captain was curing
and ordering all things with the
King that concern'd his Enterprife,
fhe made notice of it be given in
Bearn, and at *Bourdeaux,* where the
Queen her Mother was at that time.
The Attempt having failed in this
manner, the Queen conducted by
the Duke *d' Alva,* went to meet the
Court of *France* at *Bayonne :* This
Court was divided into two Factions,
almoft as great enemies one of the
other, as they were both one and the
other of the *Hugonots* their common
enemies. Although they were both
Catholicks, one of them did more
efpecially attribute to themfelves this
quality : It was that which was
headed by the Friends of the Duke
d' Alva, the firft Authors of the
Bearnifh Confpiracy. And as they
were already laying the foundations
of the League, that appeared ten
years afterwards, they lived in a perfect intelligence with the *Spaniards,*
but it was not fo with the other
Faction,

Faction, which was that of the King, and of which *Catherine de Medicis* was the chief; Arbitrarineſs, and Independency were the only end of all this Womans Actions; ſhe knew, that all inward commerce with the *Spaniard* was but ſo much ſlavery, and ſhe put no other truſt in the King her Son-in-law, and his Miniſters, then that to which ſhe was obliged by neceſſity, and her Relation to them.

In the mean time, how reſerved ſoever ſhe were, the Complices of the Duke *d'Alva* having a familiar intercourſe with her upon account of ſome other intrigues, turned ſo many Stones, and ſet ſo many Spies about her at this Interview at *Bayonne*, that at laſt they knew of a certainty that it was the Queen of *Spain* that had ruined their enterpriſe; but, they could never comprehend how this enterpriſe ſhould come to her knowledge.

The Duke *d'Alva* could not believe

lieve that so young a Woman was capable of venturing upon so bold and delicate an action.

The familiarity of this Princess with Don *Carlos* had alwayes been suspected by him, because he knew that Don *Carlos* naturally hated him.

He thought she had done nothing without advising with the Prince; and, as there are but few griefs so sensible, as that one feels for having done a wicked Action to no purpose; He took so strong a Resolution to Revenge himself on them, that at last he brought it about. Yet Don *Carlos* knew nothing of this Conspiracy before the Voyage of *Bayonne*; but, the thing being afterwards divulged, the Queen confessed the truth to him.

The Prince amazed at the horribleness of this villainous attempt, could not hinder himself from saying, in the presence of Don *John* and the Princess of *Eboli*, *That he would one day cruelly*

cruelly punish those that gave such base counsel to the King his Father.

* *Mayerne Thurquets* History of *Spain.*

* The Duke *d'Alva* was known by all the World to be the Author of the Plot, and the King did nothing without the advice of *Rui Gomez,* so that this threat could regard none but those two Ministers; and, the Princess of *Eboli* having told it to *Rui Gomez* her Husband, this Favourite judged it high time to fortifie himself against the Authority which the Princes age began now to give him.

These two Ministers did equally share the favour of the Court, only with this difference, that one might say, That the Duke *d'Alva* was the Kings Favourite, and *Rui Gomez* the Favourite of *Philip.*

This concurrence had sometimes bred some difference between them, but their common Interest reunited them upon this occasion. The Duke *d'Alva d'Alva,* who did Soveraignly govern all Military Affairs, knowing the warlike inclinations of his Prince, feared he would lessen his Authority upon the first beginnings of any War, by taking the management of it into his own hands. And he was perswaded that Don *Carlos* would never pardon him a business that was past between them some years before.

* The King had Assembled the States of *Arragon,* there to make his Son be acknowledged lawful Successor to him in the Government of the *Spaines.*

* Cabreras History of Philip the Second.

In this Ceremony it being come to the Duke *d'Alva*'s turn to swear Fidelity, the Herauld called him by his Name three times in vain. A moment afterward he came out of his rank to acquit himself of his duty, and Don *Carlos* turn'd him back very disdainfully, but the Duke excusing himself upon the multitude of business
nefs

nefs he was engaged in that day, by reafon of his Office of Great Mafter; the King obliged the Prince to accept his Submiffion. As for *Rui Gomez*, who difpofed abfolutely of the Juftice, and of the Kings Exchequer, he was afraid leaft the Prince, who naturally loved to give, fhould himfelf meddle with beftowing Favours, of which nothing fhould remain to others, but the merit of executing them. He had been Governour to Don *Carlos*, and he could never fatisfie the King (to whofe will he was wholly devoted in this employment) without ufing the Prince with the fame rigour, with which he himfelf ufed him. And, as this auftere carriage was the true caufe of Don *Carlos* his antipathy to his Father, it is neceffary here to relate fome particularities thereof, though perhaps a little mean & childifh. * Don *Carlos* being hardly entred upon his Age of Reafon, the Queen of

* *Hugo Blafius, Dutchman, in his Acroma.*

of *Bohemia* his Aunt, who lived then in *Spain*, made one of her *Pages*, whom he loved above all the rest, to be feverely chaftifed for a very light fault, and he being at that very time extreamly violent in all his paffions, complain'd to her of it with a great deal of eagernefs, and this Princefs having threatned to have him whipt, if he would not hold his peace; Don *Carlos*, whom one could not more fenfibly injure, then in ufing him like a child, was fo out of patience at this threatnirg, that he gave her a box on the Ear. As foon as fhe had left him, he began to perceive what he had done, and was much difquieted about it; when the Steward of his Houfhold prefented himfelf before him, melted into Tears. Don *Carlos*, to whom all extraordinary objects were fufpicious, in the condition he was in, asked him the fubject of his tears, and knew by him that his Father had known his Crime, and had

D   con-

condemn'd him to death : Thofe
that were prefent with him obferved,
that he received indeed this News
with fome aftonifhment, but yet
without any other mark of fear, then
asking whether there were no pardon to be had for him ? One went
prefently to the King to demand it,
and came back with this Anfwer,
That he had obtained it : but, that
he fhould not be quit without lofing
the Hand wherewith he had ftruck the
Queen. *It would be a fine thing indeed* (cryed he briskly at this Anfwer) *to fee a one-handed King.* He
was told, That it was happinefs
enough for him that the King contented himfelf with this punifhment:
But, a perfon of the Company having reprefented to him in private,
That if he fubmitted himfelf to
fome voluntary Correction, his Father might be touched with fome pitty for him; he approved that Counfel, and fent to pray the Cardinal
Spinofa to come and Whip him; a
thing,

thing, which without that confideration he would never have done.

Some years afterward, juft upon his
recovery from a Sickneſs he had had,
the King having taken him aſide to
reprove him ſeverely for ſome fault,
Don *Carlos*, who thought himſelf
blamed wrongfully*was
ſo livelily toucht with
what his Father ſaid to
him, that he fell into a
** Dicos y e-
chos,* di Phi-
lippe 2.
relapſe of his Fever at that very moment.

So harſh an Education had accuſtomed the Prince to ſee all his Sentiments and Inclinations contradicted;
and, as he was of a diſpoſition di-
rectly oppoſite to that of his Father,
he did not ordinarily govern himſelf
after ſuch a manner, as the King could
have deſired. This had often obliged *Rui Gomez* earneſtly to deſire
that he might be excuſed from wait-
ing on him any longer; he was a-
fraid that the King would at laſt, as
Fathers ordinarily do, accuſe him of

the

the little comfort he had in his Son;
but, this Favourite knew not, that
thofe people, who, like his Mafter,
think themfelves very wife, and who
brag of conftancy above all other vertues, would a thoufand times fooner
condemn their own Children, then
blame a man they have once chofen;
and, are not fo much afraid of appear-
ing unfortunate in their Families, as
unskilful in their judgments.

Rui Gomez feeing the Kings obfti-
nacy, to continue him in his charge,
had us'd Don *Carlos* with all rigour
imaginable, as it were to take away
all occafion for blaming him for his
ill conduct, fo that he judged well
that he was to fear all things from the
refentment of his Scholar; and, being
folicited by his Wife, who, under
pretence of taking care of her huf-
bands fafety, revenged her defpi-
fed favours: He did all things poffi-
ble to oblige the Duke *d'Alva* to
joyne himfelfe with him againft Don
Carlos, letting him know, how the
Prince

Prince had threatned them both.

What earneſtneſs ſoever the Princeſs of *Eboli* ſhewed to have her part
in this combination; her Huſband,
who had ſome ſuſpition of the ſince-
rity of all her officiouſneſs, did not
think it fit to entruſt her with ſo important a ſecret. She told him not
all ſhe thought ſhe knew concerning
the correſpondence betwixt Don *Carlos* and the Queen. But *Rui Gomez*,
who had a very piercing wit, making
reflection in privat upon what ſhe had
told him, had ſoon divined the reſt.
But what Idea ſoever he attempted
to make in his mind concerning this
correſpondence, he could never
for ſo perfect a conception of it, as
when he thought there was ſome love
at the bottom. A thouſand things
upon which he had not reflected at
the time when they were done,
came then into his memory. He re-
membred how he had obſerved, that
when the Queen was ſpoken of in
Don *Carlos* his preſence, that Prince

look'd

look'd upon thofe that fpake of her, as if he had feared, left they fhould obferve him at that time, and left that they faid of her, had been only to try him. In other occafions, where it feemed, that all the company difputed who fhould praife the Queen beft, Don *Carlos* praifed her not at all in his turn, as the others did: and when he muft neceffarily fpeak of her, he was always afraid of faying too little, and his mouth not accuftomed to difguife the Sentiments of his heart, could ill do a thing it was ignorant of. *Rui Gomez* confidered again, that though the Prince had no confideration for all other women, yet he appeared before the Queen with a certain fweetnefs and complaifance, that never bely'd it felf, and that render'd him uncapable of being known to thofe that were acquainted with his humour. In fine, it was not hard to believe, that the marvelous beauty of that Princefs, from which the moft infenfible were

forced

forced to turn away their eyes, and against which the oldest and wifest men of the Court had much ado to defend their reafon, fhould make upon the heart of a young Prince, who faw her familiarly every day, the impreffion it made upon all other.

Rui Gomez was confirmed in his opinion, by communicating it to the Duke *D' Alva*, from whom he thought not to hide it. And as it ordinarily happens, that when one hath difcovered one part of a fecret, the defire one hath to know the reft, makes one endeavour to Divine it, they began to doubt at that very time, that the Queen anfwered Don *Carlos* his paffion. This paffion at firft flatter'd their animofity, they were glad for fome moments that they had in their hands an infallible way of revenging themfelves upon this Prince, by difcovering his Love to his Father : But afterwards coming to make reflection upon the King's jealous humour, and upon his

natural

natural cruelty, they confidered the
ftrange extremities, to which apparently it would carry him, and were
ftricken with horrour at that thought.
How redoubtable an enemy foever
they had in the perfon of Don *Carlos*
they intended not to attaque his life,
nor ever thought themfelves capable
of fuch an intent. No body becomes
wicked all at once ; and it is not for
all forts of Souls to refolve upon a
great piece of villany the firft time it
comes into their thoughts. Vice is
arriv'd to by degrees as well as Vertue.

These two Minifters apprehended
above all things, left the Queen
fhould preoccupy her Husband's
mind about the affair of *Bearn*, fo
that afterwards he would not believe
the truth. They judged, that in the
inquietude the King was in, to know
how this enterprife had been difcover'd, he would fix himfelf upon the
firft opinion fhould be given him of
it. This Prince even defperate with
the ill fuccefs of his defign, looked
no.

no more upon the Duke *D' Alva*
with so favourable an eye as he was
wont to do, and perhaps meditated in
his own heart his open disgrace,
thereby to discharge himself of the
blame of this conspiracy. To avoid
this blow he was forced to discover
to him the truth; but because the
end of this discovery was to convince
the King, that it was not through
the Duke *D' Alva*'s fault that their
attempt had failed, the Duke did
not judge it convenient to speak to
him himself. *Rui Gomez* was not
much less suspected then he in this
affair: he had almost as great a part
in it as the Duke. They thought
then that they had need of some
third person to render them that
good office; and finding none so
proper for their purpose as *Antonio
Perez*, the Secretary of State, they
resolved to engage him in their intelligence. This man, who had no interest to hurt either the Prince or
Queen, appeared to them difficult to

be.

be gained. Nevertheless *Rui Gomez* presumed enough upon his address, to attempt the bringing it about. The thing proved much easier to him than he thought. *Perez* was passionately in love with the Princess of *Eboli*, and till then he had never been able to obtain any thing of her. He ask'd at first whether she were of the Secret; and being told that she was not, after all the refusals he knew he must make, he engaged himself to do all they desired of him. This dextrous Lover knew how furious the Princess was; he doubted not but she was almost desperate, that an intrigue of that consequence should lie hid from her, and knew she was capable of doing any thing to gratifie him that should discover it to her. *Rui Gomez* went presently to give an account of his negotiation to the Duke *d'Alva*, proud of his good success, and the most contented man in the world to have given his Wifes Gallant an infallible way of corrupt-
ing

ing her. And *Perez* knew so well how
to make use of his Secret with his Mi-
stress, that he made her buy it as dear
he pleased.

In the mean time the Queen, who
proved great with child at her return
from *Boyonne*, lay in of the *Infanta
Katharine Michaelle*, her Second
Daughter, who was since Dutchess
of *Savoy*. The Ministers who knew
the power the Queens beauty gave
her over her Husbands mind, thought
fit to take the time of her lying in
to justifie the Duke *d'Alva*, that so
they might give the King the leisure of forming a resolution upon
that, they intended he should know,
before he could have time to talk
with the Queen her self. The
charge *Perez* had of Foreign Affairs,
gave him often opportunity of entertaining his Majesty in private.
On the morrow morning he brought
in the Discourse of the Conspiracy
of *Bearn*, upon this account, that
they had heard, that the Queen of
France

of *France* seemed to be very angry
at it, and that she began to revenge
her self for it in favouring the Rebels in *Flanders*, who were then in
the first Fits of their Fury. At first
he confessed to the King, that he had
a long time hesitated to discover to
him what he knew concerning the
ill success of this Enterprise, what
Obligation soever lay upon him to
do it; but that after having well
thought upon it, he believed he
could not without a Crime continue
to be silent. After that he recount-
ed to him exactly that which the
Duke *d'Alva* had learn'd at *Bayonne*,
concerning the manner in which they
had been discovered; he added the
Discourses which Don *Carlos* had had
upon this business, in presence of
Don *John* and the Princess of *Eboli*,
against those that were concerned in
it; and he ended, in praying the
King to pardon him the Secret, he
had till then made him of those
things he could not tell him, without.

out offending in some sort the Two
Persons of the world, who (after his
own) ought to be most Sacred in his
Subjects Hearts.

This Discourse put the Kings
Mind into an extraordinary perplexity; and though as yet he did not
suspect the Queen of any thing, his
Love made him find the Union of
Sentiments, which by this Affair appeared to be between her and Don
Carlos very strange. His Mind possess'd by this first motion of Jealou-
sie, made him look with indifference
upon the Attempt they had made
upon his Authority; and the care of
his Grandeur, which was so natural
to him upon all other occasions,
gave place for this once to a more
sensible and more delicate Consideration. He observed then for the first
time his Sons Assiduity about his
Wife, and he remember'd they had
been a long while together destin'd
for each other; but he came presently to himself, and considering
the

the vertue and courage of the Queen,
he wholly condemned all such weak
Suspicions. She had already given
other marks of the love she conserved for her Country. Some time
before the difference of the Precedency of the two Crowns having
been decided at *Rome* in favour of
that of *France*, she could not so well
dissemble the joy she had of it, but
that she let go some small Testimony
of her mind. Her first Lady of Honour would have represented to her,
that she ought to be more concerned
in the discontent of her Husband upon this occasion. But the Queen answered her, That as she did not
wonder at the Kings Grief, so neither ought he to wonder at her joy;
and that for her part she was glad
to have all the world
know, that the House
* out of which she
was issued was bet-
ter, than that unto which she had al-
lied her self. The King making reflection

* Father *Hilarion* of
Cossa, in his Elogy of
this Queen.

flection upon this Difcourfe, was fully perfuaded, that what she had done againft the Enterprife of *Bearn* proceeded from the fame Principle of Affection for her Kindred; and he confidered this horrible Enterprife, in which Don *Carlos* feemed to defire to out-vie the Queen, as a Generofity pardonable in fo Young a man.

Yet though he was willing enough to be at quiet in this point, he refolved to have a clearer Knowledge of their Commerce for the time to come; but he thought there was no other Jealoufie mingled with this Refolution, than that he ought to have of his Authority. He made great Changes in the moft important Offices of the Court, that fo he might beftow upon the Princefs of *Eboli* the firft of all thofe of the Queens Houfhold, without making appear any Affectation in his Choice. The familiarity this woman had maintained with Don *Carlos* ever fince her

her Husband had been his Governour, render'd her fitter than any
other to penetrate into his Secrets.
This Confideration joyn'd to that
fhe had already reported of the
Threatnings he had made in her prefence, contributed as much as the
favour of *Rui Gomez*, to make her
be chofen by the King for this Im-
ployment. Don *Carlos*, who thought
ftill that fhe loved him, ever fince
that which had paft between them,
was not in the leaft difturbed at her
new Promotion ; and the Queen,
who knew that her Husband had
too many Friends in *France* to be ignorant of what fhe had done, was no
way furprifed by all this Change of
Offices. She imagin'd the reafon of
it at firft, and Don *Carlos* trying to
re-affure her, in anfwering for the
Princefs of *Eboli*, the Queen prefs'd
him to tell her, from whence came
the great Confidence he had in that
Woman ? But he could never get
leave of his Modefty to fatisfie her
de-

demand. Yet he perceived afterwards, that he was deceived, when he saw how carefully the Princess of *Eboli* watched them. And he not daring to complain of the Inconvenience he received by her Presence, she pleased her self wonderfully in tormenting this poor Prince. She feigned to have more Friendship for him than ever ; never failing to wait upon the Queen wheresoever she were, as soon as she knew that he was with her ; and she made as if it had been her that drew her thither. But though this Womans Vigilancy was incredible, the Queen and Don *Carlos* found a little while after an opportunity of entertaining one another in particular. The King, who was as much busied about his Escurial as one may imagine, by the fearful Expence he was at for it, invited the Queen to go see the beginnings of the proud Structure he was raising, to be an eternal monument of the Victory of S. *Quintin*. All that renewed ed in this Princesses Soul the remembrance of a Battle, that had been the fountain of all the Misfortunes of her Life, ought not apparently to be very pleasing to her.

Nevertheless she saw the Preparations that were made for Immortalizing the Memory of that Unfortunate Day, with all the Cheerfulness and Expressions of Contentment the King could have desired of her, or that he had in himself. It was in this place that the Princess of *Eboli* left the Queen and Prince alone with the King, and that the King having also left them to give his order to some of his Builders. Don *Carlos*, who could not longer live in such a Constraint, took that time to conjure the Queen to give him some assured means of talking with her in private, when it should be necessary for their common Interest so to do. He press'd her to it in so touching a manner, that she consented to him at the very first, seduced by that poor Prin-

ces

ces Defpair ; fo that they fet themfelves to find out fome probable
ways, but they all appear'd fo dangerous to the Queen, that fhe re-
folv'd never to make ufe of them,
how eafie foever Don *Carlos* would
make her believe they were. The
ftate of Affairs ftood thus, when
the Marquefs of *Bergh* and the Ba-
ron of *Monteigni*, Deputies from
Flanders, arrived at the Court. And
as their Commiffion was very dangerous, they had founded their principal hopes upon the report of the
Princes Generofity, and the good nature of the Queen. To be unhappy, was enough to deferve the Pro-
tection of that Princefs, and he that
was Vertuous had merit enough to
pretend to the Friendfhip of Don
Carlos. The Deputies reprefented to
them the fad condition of the Nobility of *Flanders*, fince the ill Offices that the Cardinal of *Cranvella*,
the principal Minifter of the Dutchefs
of *Parma*, their Governefs, had done
them,

them with the King. They exaggerated their innocence and fidelity in the paft troubles. They particularly conjured the Prince not to abandon fo many of the Emperors braveft Servants, and the moft dear objects of his tendereft affections to the violent and precipitate counfels that the jealoufie of their Vertue, and the envie of their Glory infpir'd the Duke *d' Alva* with, and, they affur'd him, that the report of his courage was the onely confolation they had in their misfortune.

Don *Carlos,* whofe natural inclination for the War had till then been fnfpended by the violence of his love, was extreamly afhamed at the hearing of this difcourfe, that he had never yet done any thing for the getting of Glory; he was yet more animated by the Letters which the Deputies prefented him from the Count of *Egmont :* This Count fummoned the Prince to make good the Promife he had given him heretofore,

tofore, to go in perſon into *Flanders* as ſoon as the War ſhould be there kindled. He repreſented the Affairs of thoſe Provinces in ſo favourable a diſpoſition for Don *Carlos*, that the Prince reſolved to make the Government of them to be given to him, and hoped, when he ſhould be there, quickly to put himſelf into a condition of undertaking all that his valour and ambition ſhould counſel him, after that the troubles ſhould be once appeaſed by his preſence. He had hardly well formed this reſolution, when the Image of the Queen preſented its ſelf to his imagination more lovely and charming then he had ever yet ſeen her, and made him doubt whether he ſhould ever have the force to leave her or no; but, making a ſerious reflection upon the State of his Affairs, he plainly ſaw, that all things ought to confirm him in his firſt reſolution.

At the beginning of their affection the extreame tenderneſs of the Princeſſes

cesses Age, had not permitted her to hide from Don *Carlos* the esteem and pitty she was toucht with for him; but afterwards, time having made her wiser, and perceiving that the testimonies of Friendship she gave him, as innocent as they were, did yet nourish his Love; she represented to him upon all occasions the ill consequences of this Passion, and the miseries to which it would expose them both. How much soever he were possessed with it, he could not hinder himself from acknowledging that she was in the right, and he durst not seem to take it ill that she lived with him for some days after a more reserved manner then ordinary. In so cruel a disturbance of mind, he thought, that he ought to make one generous effort upon himself, to deliver this Princess from an unfortunate Passion, that gave her so just causes of inquietude; And that he could not better rid himself of it, then by a long absence, and a great deal of business;

He

He thought so indeed at first, but he
quickly changed his mind at the presence of the Queen, and considering
what was the pleasure of seeing her,
he well perceived he should never resolve to see her no more. In this
thought he went and gave her an
account of what had passed between
the Deputies and him, and of the
project he had formed. He askt her
pardon a thousand times over, for
being able to think for some moments that he could live absent from
her ; but, the Queen, who aimed at
nothing but to cure him of his passion, obliged him, notwithstanding
his resistance to pursue his design of
the expedition into *Flanders*, and to
make him resolve upon it the more
easily, she represented to him, That
this Voyage would dissipate the ill
humour the King was in, through his
suspicion of their affection ; and that,
so being less observed at his return,
and more considerable and absolute,
by reason of the glory he would
doubtlessly

doubtlefly acquire, they might live together with lefs inquietude. Don *Carlos* partly perfwaded by thefe reafons, but much more by the blind obedience he had fworn to the Queen in all things, declared himfelf openly in favour of the Nobility of the Low-Countries, to the great fcandal of the Inquifitors, who held them to be almoft all infected with Herefie, and who had not yet forgotten the bufinefs of *Charles* the Fifth's Will. He made the King be told, That if he would give him the Government of thefe Provinces, he would be anfwerable to him upon his life for their obedience. It would be difficult to exprefs to what a degree *Rui Gomez* and the Duke *d' Alva* were allarm'd at this defign.

The Authority that an employment of that confequence was like to give to the Heir of the Crown, appeared to them to be their evident ruine. They judg'd, That at his return from this expedition, in which he

he would infallibly have good succefs, this Prince would be his Fathers
firft Minifter, and that by confequence they muft depend upon him.

The Duke *d'Alva* above all, who
had the fame pretenfions with *Don
Carlos*, engaged *Rui Gomez*, who was
more familiar with the King than he,
to make him confider how much this
Enterprife would raife his Son above
him in the hearts of the *Flemmings*.

Perez, without feeming to act by
confent with them, put him alfo in
fear of the ftreight League which
Don *Carlos* would doubtlefs make
with *France* by the means of the
Queen, if he were once Mafter of the
Low Countries.

Thefe *Advertifements* made all the
Impreffion they were capable of making upon the mind of a Prince naturally jealous of his Authority, and
fearful of his Sons Ambition.

The King thought no more of any
thing, but how to refufe Don *Carlos*
with a good grace; and fo that he

might not take his Refusal for an Affront.

He made him be told, that he granted his Request, and that he was ravish'd that they had both happen'd upon the same intention, but that he **was resolved** to go himself and establish him in *Flanders*, and that they would not shortly go away together for that design: that it would not be handsom for him to live securely in *Spain*, and in the mean time to expose his onely Son to the accidents of so furious a Rebellion, and that he would share the danger with him, and afterwards let him reap all the glory.

The noise of this Voyage was immediately spread abroad into all parts, by reason of the preparations the King made for it to deceive Don *Carlos*; yet no body could believe it.

In the mean time how groundless soever this noise appeared, it filled the minds of the Rebels, yet wavering with terror; and the King, to confirm it more and more, made so

con-

considerable an Expence in Equipages, that even *Bergh* and *Monteigni*, who had laughed at it till then, durst no longer doubt of its truth. The Queen and Don *Carlos* were at firſt cheated by appearances as well as the others, but they undeceived themſelves ſooner than any.

When the Equipages were finiſh'd, the King, who ſaw that people would ſoon be diſabus'd if he began not his journey, could find no other Expedient to excuſe his ſtay, but the feigning to be ſick. This pretence wrought its effect pretty well in the Countries afar off; but what care ſoever he took to make his ſickneſs be believed in his Court, and what conſtraint ſoever this poor Prince brought himſelf under, to live after a manner that might confirm the opinion he had a mind to give of himſelf, he could never deceive his Wife and his Son.

In this Conjuncture, one day that a great deal of Company that had

E 2   been

been with the Queen, and had dif-
courfed a long time about the Kings
Voyage into *Flanders*, were gone out,
Don *Carlos*, Don *John*, and the Princefs of *Eboli* being left alone with
her, at firft they made an Obfervation
altogether, How Courtiers do often
torment themfelves to divine the
Caufes and Effects of that which fhall
never be. After having fome time
laughed at thofe that had fpoken of
the Voyage, Don *Carlos* came infenfibly to laugh at the Voyage it felf,
and at the violence the King did himfelf to counterfeit the fick man ; he
faid, That *Charles* the Fifth had
made Voyages enough for himfelf
and his Son too, and that the King
would repofe both for himfelf and his
Father. The Queen did not hear
thefe words, becaufe fhe was obliged
to talk privately with fome perfons
that had bufinefs with her.

In the mean time while Don *John*
and the Princefs of *Eboli* talked foft-
ly together, Don *Carlos* in a penfive

po-

posture set himself to make a little book, in which he wrote these words in Capital Letters upon the first page, *The great and admirable Voyages of King Philip ; and in every one of the other pages of the book he wrote one of the following Titles, *The Voyage from Madrid to the Escurial, the Voyage from the Escurial to Toledo, from Toledo to Madrid, from Madrid to the Aranjuez, from the Aranjuez to the Pardo, from the Pardo to the Escurial.* And after this manner he filled the whole book with the Kings Voyages to his Houses of Pleasure, and to some of the greatest Towns in *Spain.* The Queen could not keep her self from laughing at this imagination of the Prince, how dangerous soever she thought it; but as she read this paper one came to tell her, that the King was newly fallen into a swoon, and that he was very ill. At this news she had onely the leisure to recommend the book to Don *Carlos.* The Prince,

* *Brantome* in his *Philip* the Second.

E 3   who

who would needs follow her as foon
as might be, contented himfelf to
throw it into a little Clofet, of which
he fhut the door after him. He knew
not that the Princefs of *Eboli* had falfe
keys to all the Queens Locks. He
was hardly out of the room but fhe
feifed upon his Writing; and when
fhe had feen what it was, fhe was extremely glad to have in her hands fo
confiderable a means of prejudicing
him in the Kings mind. The firft
thing fhe thought of was, how fhe
might do to keep this Paper without
any ones knowing that fhe had it. She
doubted not but the Queen had feen
the confequence it might be of, and
that fhe would feek it as foon as fhe
fhould be come back. For this pur-
pofe, without lofing a moment of time,
fhe caufed another little book to be
made in all points like that of Don
Carlos's, and which contained the fame
things. She made the Prince's writing to be perfectly well counterfeit-
ed, and put that falfe book in the
place

place of the true, which she gave her
Husband. The Queen at her return
having found this counterfeit writing
in the same place that Don *Carlos* had
told her, was in so great haste to burn
it, that she threw it into the fire almost without reading any thing in it,
no wise doubting this Cheat.

In the mean time the Kings dissem-
bling was turned into a reality. At
his coming to himself out of the
swoun he had been in, he was found
to have a strong Fever, which soon
chang'd it self into a regular Tertian
Ague : but people gave less credit to
his sickness when it was true than
they had done whilest it was but
feigned. The Rebels of *Flanders* seeing that this report had lasted so
long, doubted no more but that it
was a trick of that Princes policy.
And in that Opinion they pursued
their designs with more heat than before. This news redoubled both the
Kings Melancholy and his Sickness.
Don *Carlos* seeing that the instances

he

he fhould make to be fent into *Flanders* would but difquiet him more and more, would not renew them; but his Father, who thought him not fo difcreet, and who faw him unceffantly by his bed-fide, took his affiduity for a dumb follicitation; yet this affiduity had other reafons: The Queen never abandoning the fick man, Don *Carlos* could not fee her any where elfe, but living in his prefence with great circumfpection, and not daring almoft to fpeak to one another before him. Don *Carlos* fuffered very much by this conftraint, and their Interefts received a confiderable prejudice by it : In fo delicate a conjuncture they had a great many advices to give one another, and a great many meafures to take by confent. There was no hopes that the King would be cured of a long while, and the Phyficians affured them, that his Ague would be of a great length. The Queen and Don *Carlos* judging that there would be too much danger in writing to one

ano-

another, refolved to chufe fome faithful perfon, to whom they might fafe-
ly tell what they would have one another know. The Prince, who
thought that his Uncle Don *John* had
been their very good Friend, caft his
eyes upon him, to honour him with
this Confidence : But the Queen
thought fhe had feen divers times in
the eyes of this Uncle fomething that
fpake to her of Love ; and fhe had
obferved fome kind of officioufnefs in
the Princefs of *Eboli* for this fame
Don *John*, that fhewed there was
fome Intelligence between them.
Thefe Confiderations obliged the
Queen to make Don *Carlos* change
his defign, yet without acquainting
him with her reafons. The Prince
had not dared to propofe to her the
Marquefs of *Pofa*, his Favourite, becaufe fhe knew him not fo particularly as fhe did Don *John*. This Favorite was the moft accomplifh'd of
all the Noblemen, who had been
bred up in the Quality of Children of

Ho-

Honour, or Companions to the young
Princes. Although he had a great
deal of Vivacity, he was one of thofe
naturally regular Souls, equally capable of force and moderation. Don
Carlos, who had an excellent faculty
of difcerning, had at firft remarked
a Character of mind, fo rare amongft
young people. The Marquefs was no
lefs charmed with the ardor that Don
Carlos teftifi'd for all great and noble
things ; and they had formed for one
another an affection, hardly enough
to be found between a Prince and a
Courtier, becaufe it was founded upon nothing, but the mutual admiration of each others vertue. And as
there is no Perfonage at Court more
hard or dangerous to act than that
of Favourite to the Heir of the
Crown, the Marquefs had intreated
Don *Carlos* to make the leaft noife he
could of the Privacy wherewith he
was pleafed to honour him. So that
though they lived in a perfect union,
there appeared almoft nothing of it
in

in publick, onely that the Prince
found his Converfation much more
agreeable than that of other people,
and all the world did the like. The
Myftery they made of their Friendfhip rendered this Favourite more fit
to ferve the Queen and Don *Carlos*
upon this occafion. And not being
known to be fo much devoted to
the Prince as indeed he was, the difcourfes he fhould have with the
Queen would be much the lefs fufpected. But fhe knowing that Don
Carlos was eafily to be deceived,
would her felf examine the Marquefs
of *Pofa*, before fhe would open her
felf to him. The firft time fhe met
him at the Kings Apartment, under
pretence of fome command fhe had
to lay upon him, fhe found the means
of engaging him in a particular converfation. His prudence appeared to
her fo great, that fhe was even
charmed therewith. He was not lefs
taken with the Queens wit ; and his
natural moderation was never of fo

great

great use to him, as upon this occasion. Considering the manner in
which this Princess made her self
known to him in this Discourse,
which was heightened by the lustre
of her Beauty, and her charming
Sweetness, any other man that had
not been so absolutely Master of himself as he was, would doubtless have
fallen in love with her. But though
he did not do so, they could not hinder one another in the rest of the
Commerce they had together, from
conceiving for each other all the
esteem and friendship they both me-
rited.

We are always apt enough to believe, that people divine those secret
sentiments that are truly ours; but
we fear not being suspected of those
we have not. The Queen, who
troubled her head about nothing,
but hiding those that Don *Carlos*
had for her, and who had none for
the Marquess of *Posa*, but what were
very consonant to reason, took not so
                                    much

much care as she ought to have done to conceal them. She feared not being suspected of having any Criminal ones for that Favourite. The Marquess, that he might answer her goodness as he ought was often engaged to shew more eagerness for her service, than the exact Rules of Prudence would have permitted to be seen. And as they were neither of them without Enemies, this Carriage quickly made a noise in the world. But they not imagining it would so do, because they were conscious of their own innocency, hardly took any notice thereof.

In the mean time the King was cured, and the Queen proved with child. At first he was extremely glad of it, whether it were out of the hopes of having another Son besides Don *Carlos,* or that as yet doubting of the perfect establishment of his Health, this Greatness appeared to him to be an assured mark of it; but his joy was not of long continuance.

The

The Minifters, who were afraid of
the fecret favour of the Marquefs
of *Pofa*, ordered the matter fo, that
the Queens Commerce with this
Marquefs came quickly to the knowledge of the King. This fufpicious
Prince, at the very firft notice thereof, had his mind troubled with jealoufie, and not finding his reckon-
ing in fome account of time, he
was pleafed to make upon the ftate
of his Wife's Greatnefs,
* did not ftick to think
the Marquefs guilty of
a Crime, that would
have drawn upon him more Envy
than all his Vertues. This thought
made a ftrange diforder in his heart.
All the Graces, both of Body and
Mind, that Nature had fo liberally
beftowed on this Unfortunate Favourite, and that were capable of
touching the moft Barbarous Soul,
rendred him by fo much the more o-
dious to the King, as that Prince confidered no more all thofe precious

* *Mayerne Tur-
quett*, in his Hi-
ftory of *Spain*.

Ta-

Talents but as fo many Criminal Charms that had feduced his Wife's Heart. Neverthelefs, how dangerous foever this Difpofition of the Kings Mind were, perhaps his Reafon would have returned to him, had it not been for a thing that happened at that very time, and which made him fully believe what he did but fufpect before.

* Among other pub-
lick Teftimonies of joy that were made for his Recovery, there was a Magnificent Tournament, in which every Cavalier was obliged to declare himfelf for fome Lady of the Court, and to wear her Colours. The Evening before this great day, the Marquefs of *Pófa* happening to be in the Queens Chamber, which was full of Company, fhe made him name to her all the Ladies that had Knights to defend their Beauties. The Prince and Don *John* were the onely men that could declare

* Mr. *Mezeray*, in his great Hiftory.

clare themselves to be hers ; and
they not having done it , perhaps
through fear of discovering something of what they had in their
Souls, it so fell out , when they
had done speaking, that the Queen
was the onely person that had no
body to run for her. She observed it her self, and complaining of
it in a jesting way, the Marquess,who
knew he might use any sort of plea-
santry with her, told her with a wonderful serious look,*That she must blame
Nature for it ; and that if she had been
beautiful like the others, she would doubtless have found some Knight as they had
done.*

All the Company applauded this
Raillery, and the Queen answered
him as seriously as he had spoken,
*That to punish him for his insolency,
she commanded him to be her Knight;
that so he might have the shame of ser-
ving the least beautiful of all the Ladies.*

This

This Gallantry was publick, and all the People of the firſt Quality at Court were witneſſes of it.

Yet the King could not keep himſelf from thinking that there was ſome Myſtery in it, and that this Converſation was an artifice of the Queen to give her Lover an aſſured means of declaring himſelf for her with impunity. Yet he was not at firſt fully confirmed in this opinion; but on the morrow morning, when he ſaw the Marqueſs enter into the Liſts, carrying for his Device upon his Shield a Sun in its higheſt Elevation, with theſe words, *Nothing can ſee me without being burnt.*

This Prince was fully perſuaded of the ſad thought that ſtuck in his mind. The unfortunate Knight won the Prize of the firſt Courſes, and though that were ordinary enough with him, the King at this time took his Addreſs for an effect of his Love; and this Imagination touch'd him ſo to the quick, that he could not endure

dure to let the Jufting be finifhed, and he feigned that he found himfelf ill, to have a pretence of breaking them off, and to hinder people from perceiving the Fury into which this Innocent Spectacle had put him.

At firft he refolved to give the Marquefs of *Pofa* his Death in fuch a manner, that neither he nor the Queen could be ignorant of its caufe; but *Rui Gomez*, whom he confulted about it, made him fee the Confequences of a bufinefs of that nature, and that was like to make fo much noife. He let him know the ftreight Friendfhip that was between Don *Carlos* and this Marquefs, and made him comprehend that there was nothing that was not to be feared from the refentment of the Prince for the lofs of a Perfon fo dear to him, if once he came to know the Authors of it.

* *Mayerne Turquett.* * He contented himfelf to have the Marquefs Stab'd

fome

fome time afterwards one night in the Streets, as he was retiring himfelf from Court ; the better to keep the truth of the bufinefs from being infpected, when the Affaffines faw him dead, they feigned in the prefence of his Attendants, that they had taken him for another man. The Queen refented, as she ought, the lofs of fo perfect a Friend, and she faw at the very firft all she was confequently to fuffer by it. As for Don *Carlos*, he could not at firft difcover the true caufe of it, but afterwards he confidered the little appearance there was, that a Man fo well known as the Dead Man was, should be taken for another. On the other fide, he faw, that there was no body but his Father that durft undertake fuch an Attempt ; fo that he did not hefitate no more than the Queen to divine, who was the Author of it. In the mean time they neither of them miftrufted, that it

was

was of the Marquefs that the King
had been Jealous, and imagining rather that which was like to have
been, then that which really was; they
thought that this Favourite had been
killed as a Confident, and not as a
Lover, and that they were difcovered.
In this opinion, confidering the
Kings unmeafurable paffion for his
Wife, his averfion for the Prince,
and his natural inclinaiion to fhed
blood, they judged themfelves loft.

And they thought, that the King
being well affured that they could not
efcape his vengeance, had begun by
this Affaffinate, that fo he might
make them feel it the longer.

There is nothing fo fecret in Princes Courts that is not difcovered by
fome people, which one doth not di-
ftruft. Don *Carlos*, much about this
time, fitting down one day at the Ta-
ble, found under his Plate a Paper,
which contain'd thefe words.

There are fome very juft Counfels
which

*which yet are not given, but one comes
not out of desperate affairs, without extraordinary resolutions. Those, in
whom Heaven hath put such qualities,
as are to render a great many others
happy, besides those that possess them,
are obliged to accomplish their destiny,
which prevails over all other Obliga-
tions. Generous Souls perish not but
for want of having an opinion bad
enough of the wicked. That Patience,
which abandoneth the days of a Gallant man to the violence of his Enemies, is weakness, baseness of heart,
crime, and not vertue. Humanity for
those that have none, is the most dangerous sort of folly.*

In the mean time the Prince resolved to try one innocent way, before
he would have recourse to the ut-
most extremity. This way was, to
renew with great earnestness the request he had made to be sent into
Flanders, where the state of Affairs
demanded a more present, and speedy
remedy

remedy then ever; He did it in termes, that made the King comprehend, that he would have what he defired, and that there was no fafety to refufe him; He judged it his beft way to exprefs his mind in this abfolute manner, for he thought, that if he were difcovered, he had nothing more to Hufband, and if he were not, it might happen that the King, follicited by his jealoufie, and affrighted by this imperious way of proceeding, would grant him any thing in the World to be rid of him.

This unfortunate Father, whofe mind was more free to fee the confequences of his Cruelty, after he had fatisfied it, was again fallen into his natural timidity: he faw plainly that he muft neceffarily fend an Army into *Flanders*, and he was afraid of irritating Don *Carlos* his refentment, yet frefh for the death of his Friend, if he refufed him the Command of his Army, which

he

he demanded in such high termes.

Rui Gomez, who had found the King so resolute in the business of the Marquess, was not a little astonished to see him so unresolved in an occasion of much greater importance. The Interest which this Minister had in his Masters welfare, made him look with dread upon the weakness of that Prince who was going to put the Arms into his Sons hands, wherewith he was like to have his own Throat cut the first.

As there is no reason so strong as fear, to oblige the most unstable spirits to determine themselves, the King was ready to resolve himself in favour of Don *Carlos*.

Rui Gomez, who saw it well, knew not how to hinder it, but having a very present wit, he bethought himself all of a sudden of that Book of the Kings Voyages, which his Wife had found in the Queens Close, written with Don *Carlos* his hand, and which he had lookt upon ever since as a
Toy,

Toy, which might yet produce some
great effect, if it were employed with
discretion ; And, now he thoght he
had found the occasion of using
it.

He told the King, That he thought
himself obliged to let him know a
little thing, that till then he had
not thought worthy of acquainting
him with, but which in the present
conjuncture, would help him much
the better to guess at the Genius and
Sentiments of his Son.

The King to whom this affair appeared of greater consequence then
Rui Gomez made shew of thinking it,
would needs examine the Book himself; and, knowing it to be of his
Sons own Writing, he entred into a
profound thoughtfulness, in which
this Minister thought it best to leave
him.

After that he was a little come to
himself, from the first trouble of
Mind, into which so bloody a Raillery, made by two persons so dear unto
him,

him, had at firſt caſt him ; his antient
ſuſpitions of *Don Carlos*, his love for
the Queen, awakened themſelves in
his Soul with more violence then ever.
He could not comprehend that a Wife
and a Son ſhould divert themſeves in
that manner, at the coſt of a Father
and a Husband that was their King,
without living in the moſt Criminal
familiarity : But, the Marqueſs of *Poſa*
coming preſently into his mind, he
could not believe that the Queen was
in love with them both, eſpecially,
Don *Carlos* and the Marqueſs being
ſo united as they were; and, he concluded, that it muſt neceſſarily be,
that one was the Lover, and the other
the Confident : Yet, what effort of
wit ſoever he could make, he could
never determine in himſelf which was
the Lover. But, which ſoever of the
two it were, he ſtill found that the
death of the Marqueſs was but too
juſt, and that Don *Carlos* was equally
culpable.

G   However

Howe're the matter went, he would
not authorize the Railleries *his* Son
made upon his manner of life, by gi-
ving him the means of leading so different a one in *Flanders*.

If this Prince, who had yet done
nothing, had the boldness to treat
his Father with so much contempt,
what would he not have dared to
have done, if Fortune had been favourable to his ambition.

The King made him be bold, That
in the fearful disorder in which *Flanders* was, he thought he could not
send him thither, without exposing
his life to inevitable danger; but that
the Duke *d'Alva* should go thither
with a powerful Army within a short
time, and that as soon as his Army
should have rendred his side the
strongest, he should be free to do
whatever he would desire.

This refusal fully confirmed the
Prince in the opinion he had, that his
ruine was resolved upon, so that he
rendred himself to the instances that
the

the Rebels of *Flanders* had been a long time making to him by the Count of *Egmont* and their Deputies, to go and put himself at their head. They promised him, That if he would grant them a few things, that were very reasonable, they would obey him with more fidelity, then the Catholicks obey'd the King.

Don *Carlos* doubted not, but that if he were once Master of this Revolted People, the King would abandon to him the rest of *Flanders*, though it were but to hinder him from possessing himself of it by force, as it would be easie for him to do.

The Marquess of *Bergh* and *Monteigni* had several Conferences with him upon this Project, and they took together so just and so solid Measures for the executing of it, that they could not fail of success, provided, that the Prince conserved to himself the liberty of Acting. It was that to which they exhorted him prin-

cipally

cipally, and if he had taken their
Counsel, he had began his journey at
at that very time. But, Don *Carlos*
judged, that there would be too
much rashness in declaring himself
after that manner, before he had
established the correspondency that
were necessary for him : but, he promised them, that in the mean time, he
would make use of such powerfull
precautions for the safety of his person, that he should be able to give
. . . . . them a good account of
*. * Mr de* it. Besides, a Coffer
I bou. filled with Fire Armes,
which he made be set at
his Beds-head ; he caused some little
Pistols to be made, of a new Invention, to carry alwayes about him,
without being seen. And that he
might hinder himself from being
surprized in his sleep, he commanded a famous French Artist, who
workt at the *I scurial*, to make a kind
of Lock for his Chamber that could
not be open'd but on the inside, and
he

he put every night under his Bolster two Swords and a Case of Pistols.

Whilst this unfortunate Prince hastened perhaps his undoing, by the sole opinion he had that he was undone; his Enemies forgot nothing to take from him alwayes of reconciling himself with his Father. The King had not yet seen the Queen in private, since the death of the Marquess of *Posa*, and they feared that all their labour would prove to be in vain, if he saw her again, and that she would easily take out of his heart all that which they had put into it. Although it might happen that what they feared should not come to pass, yet it was possible that it might come to pass: And considering the consequence of which the thing was to them, they ought not to put any thing to the hazard.

To take from this Princess the occasion of undoing in one night, that which had cost them so much care and time, they bethought themselves

of

of a means which would appear ridiculous, if it had not succeeded.

* At the Voyage which the Court of *France* made along the River of *Loire* in the time of *Francis* the Second, there ran a report, That his Servants sought out little Children to bathe that young King in their blood, whom they feigned to be troubled with the Disease which is cured by this strange remedy : Nay, and there were some persons that went some dayes journeys before the Court, and who examined carefully the children of the places where it was to pass, to observe those that they found fit for the use which the Physicians were to make of them. These unknown persons spread so general a fear in all their way, that all the people thought no more of any thing, but how to hide from them that which they pretended to seek.

* *Mayerne Turquet, La Plauches History; La Places Memoire; Monsieur de Mezerai; Le Laboureur; Diogenes, &c.*

The

The Queen-Mother having discovered the Authors of this horible report, made some of them be taken;
They discovered at their death by
whom they had been set on; but,
those which received their Confessi-
on, judge it not safe for them to
divulge it.

If the continual infirmities of the
King made so extravagant a calumny
be so easily believed among his own
People, it's not hard to judge of the
effect it produced in Forreign Countries, where those sorts of Newes alwayes find more credit then in the
places where they are done. The
King of *Spain* testified a great deal
of trouble about it. He was afraid
that his Wife had some secret disposition to this same illness, which often
an hereditary distemper. The Small
pox which she had had since that, was
accompanyed with some equivocall
accidents that were common with
that infirmity. They resolved to
make the King believe, that she had

had

had some others, much more dangerous then the former at this last greatness. And as he had a mind very easie
to be wrought upon in that which
concern'd his health, they thought
that if they strengthned this story by
the testimony of some persons not to
be suspected, it would be enough to
hinder him from ever seeing his Wife
again in private. The Princess of
Eboli was to give him the first notice
of it, she was obliged so to do, by
the fidelity she had promised him, in
the employment she had about the
Queen. And that same French-wo-
man for whom Den *John* had for-
merly made appear some inclination,
was to confirm that which the Princess should say. This young woman
was one of those meddling spirits,
born for the management of an intrigue ; and she was inconsolable, that
all the favour she had with her Mi-
stress, had never been able to interest
her in any important confidence.
The Princess of *Eboli* commanded
Don

Don *John* to counterfeit the Lover
a fecond time, by that means abfolutely to gain to them this dangerous
Perfon. This Prince, who found fome
fweetnefs in troubling the Kings
happinefs, obeyed with great eagernefs. But the young woman, much
offended by the coldnefs he had had
for her, would not believe him ex-
cept he gave her fome extraordinary
affurances. Don *John*, in hafte to
finifh his bufinefs, did not ftick to
make her a promife of Marriage, upon
condition that fhe fhould tell the King
whatfoever they would have her.
The thing fucceded much more eafily
then they had hoped. The King,
whofe Love was already changed into indignation, ran blindly into the
Snare they had laid for him. The
Duke d' *Alva* who had deferred his
Voyage, to attend the Succefs of this
Artifice, went a way for *Flanders* the
day after. He took leave of Don *Carlos*
in termes that were conformable to
the anfwere which the King had made

to

to that Princes laft requeft : And Don *Carlos* treated the Duke very ill for fear of having his defigns fufpected, if he had appeared too calme in an occafion, which ought to touch him fo fenfibly.

In the mean time this Prince received from all parts the beft newes he could have wifhed for. The Prince of *Orange* and the Admiral *de Chatillion*, with whom he was to confult upon all he had to do, encouraged and haftned him by their Letters, whether it were to ferve him or to undo him, God knows. The revolted party in the *Low-Countries*, abfolutely confiding in his generofity, demanded of him no conditions. But that which perfected his refolution, was, the affurance of a confiderable Fleet, which the Grand Signior was to fend upon the coaft of *Flanders*, to favour all his defigns. But as his principal hope was founded upon this affiftance, it is neceffary to confider this bufinefs in its firft beginnings.   * At

* At the time that Queen *Mary* was Governess of the *Low-Countryes* for the Emperour her Brother, a certain *Jew*, that was a *Portuguez* by birth, named *John Miquez*, for whom she had a very particular esteem, ravish'd in her Court a young Lady of the first Quality, and *of an extraordinary beauty. The King of *Spain*, who protected the kindred of this fair person, having made the Ravisher be driven out of all the States of Christendom, where he sought for a Sanctuary, he retir'd himself to *Constantinople*, and from thence into *Caramania*, to the Court of *Selimus*, eldest Son of *Soliman the Magnificent*. This young Prince, who was confin'd to that Countrey by his Father, according to the custome of their House, had no other care then how to pass the time as well as he could in the midst of pleasures and divertisements, in expectation of the Empire. *Miquez*, amongst other Talents, possess'd the Art

Mr. de Thou, Strada, &c.

Art of diverſifying theſe pleaſures
after a hundred ſeveral manners, of
which every one had a new and particular charm. He knew how to give
them that ſweet point, which makes
them be felt with ſo much delight,
and which is ſo eaſily blunted by an
unskilful hand. And having culti-
vated, by a long and curious exer-
ciſe, the Genious he had for that Science, he had carri'd it to a perfection
infinitely beyond the imagination of
Vulgar. Swell'd with pride for his
skill in theſe rare Arts, he doubted
not, but he ſhould in a ſhort time
have the firſt place in the favour of
a Prince like *Selimus*, who under-
ſtood perfectly the worth of volu-
ptuouſneſs. This man knew, that
thoſe ſervices which make the greateſt
noiſe, are not always thoſe that
are moſt ſenſible to the hearts of
Sovereigns. It ſeems, that thoſe
one renders them publick, are ſuffi-
ciently recommended by the glory
that follow them; but they alone

can recompence thofe which are known by no body but themfelves. The fuccefs furpaffed *Miquez* his hopes, and *Solyman* dying in this conjuncture, the *Jew* faw himfelf by thefe glorious ways the declared Favourite of the greateft Prince upon earth. This high degree of power quickly gave him the occafion of fatisfying the defire of revenge, which the perfecution that he had fuffered had engraven in his heart againft the King of *Spain*. One day as he was in a debauch with the Sultan, that Prince having admir'd the excellency of the Wine of *Cyprus*, the *Jew* fell a laughing at him, for the paffion he fhewed for a Liquor that grew out of his Empire; and he told him that he ought to fpare it more then he did, becaufe he bought it. *Selimus* a little netled with this raillery, fwore that he would take *Cyprus* that very year; and he added, ftriking the *Jew* upon the fhoulder with his hand, that becaufe *Miquez* loved that marvellous Wine

no

no lefs then he, he declared him, from the time they were fpeaking, King of that Ifland, which yet, he faid was but a fmall part of the gratitude he owed him.

At the time that all things difpo-fed themfelves for this enterprife, the Moors of *Granada* were prepa-ring that famous rifing, which brake forth foon afterwads. They fent their Deputies to the *Ottoman* Court, to beg its affiftance. *Miquez* preferring the pleafure of revenging himfelf, before that of making him-felf a King, undertook their bufinefs with to much heart, that he made his Mafter refolve to fend to their fuc-cour the re-doubtable Navy that was then Equipping, for the conqueft of the Kingdom that was deftin'd to be his. He had concerved great cor-refpondencies in *Flanders*, and he pre-fently gave advice to the Confiftory of *Antwerp* of this important diver-fion. This Confiftory, which was the principal Council of the Rebels., having

having received at the fame time the news of Don *Carlos* his Engagement in their favour, fent word thereof to *Miquez* : and to teftifie how much truft they put in the Prince, they fent him the Jews Difpatches, and his Cipher, that fo he might himfef negotiate with him at *Conftantinople*, if he thought it ufeful for the common intereft fo to do. Don *Carlos* defired, for the greater furety: that this Fleet, which was to take Land upon the Coaft of *Granada*, might be landed in *Flanders*. He wrote of it to the *Ottoman* Court, and *Miquez* anfwer'd him, that the *Bafhaw* of the Sea had a fecret Order to do whatfoever the Prince fhould command; whether it were that the thing were true, or that they had onely a defign to make it believed, thereby to engage Don *Carlos*, at what price foever it were.

About this time, one night, as he was at play with his Uncle, at the Queen's Lodgings, they had fome difference between them, in which

Don

Don *John*, who was vex'd at his los,
was carried by his paffion to fay fome
things againft the Prince, beyond the
bounds of liberty that this Play could
give him with the Son of his King.
Don *Carlos*, who knew himfelf fuf-
ficiently, anfwered him in few words,
with moderation enough; but yet in
terms that feem'd to reproach him
with the defect of his birth, to make
him remember his duty. Don *John*
touched in fo fenfible apart, was out-
raged therewith, to the point of
answering the Prince,

* *Brantome* in his Difcourfe of *Philip* 2d.

* That if it was true in-
deed that he was a Ba-
ftard, but that which
comforted him for it, was, that he had
a better Father then he. This word
drew out all Don *Carlos* his patience:
he treated his Uncle fo rudely, that
on the morrow morning there ran a
report, that he had given him a box
on the ear. The Queen and the Princefs of *Eboli*, who were prefent, had
much ado to hinder them from coming

ing to blows. The Queen especially, who was frighted with every thing in this conjuncture, and as if she had had some secret presentiment of the consequences of this quarrel, employ'd all her Authority to oblige them to make up the difference upon the place: but it was not done with an equal sincerity on both sides.

The King, to be faithfully instructed of whatsoever passed at the Queen's apartment, had linked himself in a streight commerce with the Princess of *Eboli* : This woman had obliged Don *John* to observe the Prince's actions more narrowly then ordinary, ever since the death of the Marquess of *Posa*.

It was easie to *Don John* to acquit himself of this Commission. The Prince, who thought him his best friend, had told him something of his design in general terms; but though Don *John* had forgot nothing to know the particulars of it, he had not as yet been able to learn any thing

of

of them. Yet fince their difference, the defire of revenge had made him fo clear-fighted, that what care foever Don *Carlos* took to furnifh himfelf with Arms in fecret, Don *John,** what by addrefs, and what by money, difcovered it at the end. The King judged well, that the Prince did not take all thefe precautions, to have them always about him, he comprehended prefently, that his Son muft either have fome defign to fteal away, or to do him fome violence. He knew not which of the two to think, when Don *Raimond de Taxes,* Mafter of the Poft-Office, came to advertife him, that a *French-man* belonging to the Queen, had demanded of him very fecretly three Horfes, to be ready to go away at the beginning of the night. This advice drawing the King out of the doubt in which he was, caft him into a greater, which was, whether he fhould content himfelf to make the Prince be watched,

* *Hiftoria de* D. Juan d' Auftria.

fo

so that he could not possibly escape; or whether he should all of a sudden make him to be arrested. But *Perez* bringing to him at the same time the news of the *Moors* rising, which he had newly received; the King affrighted by so many unhappy conjunctures, resolved to assure himself of his Son's person.

It was true, that the Prince's departure was resolv'd upon for that night : he had received a few days before some news out of *Flanders*, that permitted him no longer to delay. The Counts *d' Egmont* and *de Horn*, trusting to the innocence of their intentions in their past carriage, and to the merit of their services, had delivered themselves into the hands of the Duke *d' Alva*, who made them be put in prison, and a little while after cut off their heads. So manifest a piece of treachery had cast the Rebels into despair, and their Leaders, seeing there was no more safety for them but in their Arms, made Don
Carlos

Carlos easily see, in acquainting him
with these things, that it would shortly be too late to help them. He wrote
forthwith to Don *Gracia Alvarez
Oforio*, who was to be the companion
of his flight, to come incontinently
to him. The Prince had sent him to
Sevil, there to receive a considerable
sum of money: but not having time
to make use of all the diligence requi-
red, he brought him
about an hundred and
fifty thousand Crowns.
As Don *Carlos* retired
himself from the Queens-Lodgings,
Rui Gomez walk'd with him, to give
him an account on the King's part of
the news they had received from
Granada. This Minister entertain'd
him so late, that the Prince seeing he
had not night enough left to go so far
as he desired, before his flight could
be discover'd, thought it his best way
to put it off till the morrow. *Rui
Gomez* retir'd himself, after he had
seen him in bed; but being ignorant
of

* *Cabrera's Hifto-
ry of Philip 2d.
Hiftoria de Dom.
Juan d'Auftria.*

of the change of his * resolution, he set some of *A r. de Thou,*
his most faithful and reso-. *Mayenne &c.*
lute men at all the avenues of the
Prince's apartment. It had been to be
wish'd for the King's justification, that
Don *Carlos* had been taken in at-
tempting to escape.

But when they had waited two or
three hours, without seeing any appearance of his coming out, the King
resolved to pass on, not thinking that
he ought to hazard all things for a
formality. Don *John* had observed
the manner in which his Chamber
door was shut, and whilst Don *Carlos*
was yet at the Queen's Chamber, the
King had commanded the maker of
that extraordinary Lock, to spoil the
spring of it some how or other, that
so it might no more shut so close,
but that it might be open'd on the
outside. Whatsoever this Workman
could do, the Spring made a great
noise in opening; but the Count of
Lerma, whom the King made enter
first

firſt into the room, found the unfortunate Prince ſleeping ſo ſoundly,
that he had the leiſure to take away
the Swords and Piſtols that were
under his Bolſter, without waking of
him. After this, the Count ſate down
upon a Coffer that ſtood by his bed-
ſide, and in which Don *John* thought
the Fire-Arms were kept. Then the
King judging by the Connt of *Lerma*'s ſilence, that he had done what
he ought to do, entred himſelf into
the Chamber, preceded by *Rui Gomez*, the Duke of *Feria*, the great
Commander, and Don *Diego de Cor-
duba*, all armed with Swords and Piſtols. The Prince being awakened
with much ado by *Rui Gomez*, as ſoon
as he had opened his eyes, cried out
that he was dead. The King told
him, That all they did was for his
good. But Don *Carlos* ſeeing that he
ſeized on a Box full of Papers, that
was under his bed, entred into ſo furious a deſpair, that he was going to
throw himſelf, all naked as he was,
into

into a great Fire-pan full of Coals, which the extremity of the cold had obliged his servants to leave lighted in his Chimney. They were fain to draw him from it by force, and he appeared inconsolable, that he had not had the time to smother himself in it. They presently unfurnish'd his Chamber, and instead of so many magnificent things, which they took out of it, they put into it, for its only furniture, a scurvy Ground-pallet. None of his Officers after that time ever appeared in his presence. His Guards never let him go out of their sight.

* They caused a mourning Suit to be made for him, and he *Matthieu his History of France. Mr. de Thou, &c.*

was no more waited upon, but by men clothed in the same dress, and who were unknown to him. This unfortunate Heir of so many Crowns saw no more any thing about him, which did not represent to his eyes the frightful image of death.

In

In the mean time the King faw the
defigns and intelligence of his Son by
the Papers which he had feized.   He
was aftonifhed at the greatnefs of the
danger he had run ; but, he was yet
more touched, when amongft feveral Letters * of the
Queen's   Hand-wri-
ting he found one,
which appeared to
him the moft Paffio-
nate and moft Amorous in the world.
It was that which the Marquefs of *Pofa* had carried to *Alcala*, and which
Don *Carlos* would never be perfwaded to reftore.   As the Queen had
written it in the firft tranfport of her
grief, for the Mortal Accident that
had befallen that Prince, fhe did not
think any confequence could be
drawn from what fhe could fay to a
Man, whofe life was defpaired of; or,
that it could produce any other confequence then to make him die more
contentedly. So that fhe had abandon'd her felf to all her tendernefs in
writing

* *Mayern's Hi-
ftory of Spain, Du-
plex's* Hiftory of
France, &c.

writing it, and had in it expreſſed the deareſt and moſt ſecret ſentiments of her heart, with all the violence that ſo lamentable an occaſion could inſpire. Yet it was without any Paſſionate expreſſions that could intereſt her honour, or ſo much as offend her Duty.

But the King drew very different conſequences from it : The fury he conceived for it was at firſt accompanied with ſo lively a grief, that it would perhaps have bereaved him of his Life, if the deſire of revenge (ſo natural in thoſe occaſions) had not preſerved it.

But reflecting preſently in himſelf, That he was Maſter of thoſe that had ſo cruelly offended him, this agreeable thought made a barbarous joy ſucceed to the rage he had in his Soul, which changed his tormenting deſpair into a tranquility full of horrour. The ſame day *Monteigni* was clapt in priſon, to leave ſome time after his head upon a ſcaffold, and

H the

the Marquess of *Bergh* in favour of *Rui Gomez* his ancient friend had leave to poison himself. The intimacy of these Two Noble-men with Don *Carlos* was known to all the world. They were both, as well as he, declared enemies of the Cardinal *Spinosa* Inquisitor General, and this Enmity was enough in *Spain* to make a man suspected for his Religion. They accused this *Prelate* to be the Authour of all those violent Councels that the King had taken against their country, but the Cardinal accused them themselves of having made several Packets of *Calvin's Catechismes* he brought out of *France*, by the help of a *Passport* from Don *Carlos*. All the passionate proceedings of this Prince against the Inquisitors about the will of *Charles* the fifth, were not as yet forgotten. All these things joyned together did strangely dispose the people to believe the Innocent Prince engaged in the new opinions, of which he had never so much as heard
any

any body speak; The King saw well
that there was nothing but Religion
that could make so strange an action,
as that he had done be endured. He
doubted not but that with these
favorbale dispositions, and the proofs
he had of his Son's intelligences, he
could, if he would, Sacrifice him
with impunity to his revenge. In this
belief, he put into the hands of the
Cardinal *Spinosa* all the Originals he
had found in Don *Carlos* his Cabinet,
excepting onely the Queen's Letters.
He established the Inquisitors, So-
vereign Judges between his Son and
him; and he protested, he would
wholly refer himsef to their Judg-
ment. He knew that the choler of
that sort of people never dies, and
that he should find their resentment
against the Prince as violent, after
several years of interval since their
quarrel, as if it had been but a week
before.

Although the King had made ri-
gorous prohibitions to write of the
impri-

† *Cabrera's History of Philp 2d.*
Hist. D. *Juan.*

* imprisonment of Don *Carlos* into Forreign Countries, the news of it was soon spread abroad. The most part of the Princes of Christendom begg'd his pardon ; the Empress especially wrote concerning it to the King her Brother, with all earnestness imaginable. Her eldest Daughter had been promised a long while before to the Prince of *Spain.* The King who feared all that might give more liberty and credit to his Son, had always deferred the accomplishment of this Marriage. Amongst other pretences of this delay, he made a report be spread, that since Don *Carlos* his fall at *Alcala*, the Physicians did not think he could ever have any children. This report passed for an Artifice, and the Empress her self did in no wise believe it. In the mean time, it was so much the easier to the King to draw this Alliance out into length, because Don *Carlos* did not press it

so

ſo much as he might have done:
How advantagious ſoever it were for
his deſigns, he made a ſcruple of
marrying a Princeſs that he could
not love. The Empreſs, who knew
not the ſecret of his heart, could find
but this one Match worthy of her
eldeſt Daughter : and not thinking
the Queen of *Spain's* death ſo near as
it was, ſhe did not foreſee, that this
Daughter was to take the place of
that unfortunate Queen, and that the
King her Brother, as it were by a
kind of fatality, was to marry all the
Princeſſes, that had been promiſed to
Don *Carlos.* The King, who ſaw further then ſhe, took a particular care
to manage her upon this occaſion,
* and to juſtifie him-
ſelf in her opinion. *Crabrera's Hiſto-
In the mean time ry of Philip 2d.
this news caſt the Rebels of *Flanders*
and *Granada* into a deſpair, that produced very bloudy effects : and they
would yet have been more cruel, if
the *Turks* had kept their word ; but

Miquez

Miqeuz judged not, that without the support of the Prince of *Spain*, he ought to hazard the *Ottoman* Fleets in places so far from all possibility of help, in case of disadvantage. He yielded himself to the opposition, that other Ministers of that Court made against the continuation of his enterprise; and it was changed into that of *Cyprus* where he made known, by the marvellous services he rendred, * that all his Genius was not shut up within the Walls of the *Seraglio*; and that the love of pleasure doth not always render those that are possess'd with it, incapable of great actions.

* *Cabrera's* History of *Philip* 2d Mr. *de Thou, Strada,* &c.

In the mean time the Inquisitors formed the Process of the unfortunate Don *Carlos*, with an incredible affection and diligence. Their ancient animosities against him appear'd so openly, that nothing but the interest of Religion, which was mingled with them

(143)

them, could have made them be supported * They sent to look among the Archives of *Barcelona*, for

* *Cabrera* Hist. de D. *Juan*.

the criminal procefs that Don *John* the fecond of that name, King of *Arragon*, had caufed heretofore to be made againft Don *Carlos* Prince of *Viana*, his eldeft Son. They made this procefs be tranflated out of *Catalonian* into *Caftilian*, to ferve them all at once, both for a Model and a Prefident. The bufinefs was propofed to the Inquifition, under the fpecies of *Lewis* the Eleventh, Dauphin of *France*, and King *Charles* the Seventh his Father. And all their opinions being the fame, one may judge of them by that of the famous Doctor *Mavarra*, which is inferted * in the Hiftory of *Philip* the Second.

* *Cabrera* in the Hiftory of *Philip* 2d.

He decides, that a King, who difcovers, that the prefumptive Heir of his Crown will go out of his States,

H 4 ought

ought to make him be ſtopped by force, if his evaſion can be a ſubject of diviſion in the Kingdom, and that the enemies of the State are in a capacity of drawing any conſiderable uſefulneſs from it; but eſpecially if thoſe enemies are Hereticks, and that there be the leaſt reaſon to fear or ſuſpect that this Prince favours them. The Sacrafice that the King made of his natural affection, to the repoſe of the State, was preſented by the Inquiſitors. Before the obedience of *Abraham*, * They compared, all with one voice, this Prince to the Eternal Father, who had not ſpared his ownSon for the ſalvation of Mankind

* Mr le *Labourer* upon *Caſtalnau*, in his Ch. of Don *Carlos*.

.His Trial could not be long before Judges that were ſo wel diſpoſed. The ſole Letters of the Admiral *de Chatillon*, the Prince of *Orange*, the Count of *Egmont*, the Conſiſtory of *Antwerp*, and of *John Miquez* were ſufficient

cient to forme his Sentence, and Don *Carlos* was Condemn'd to perpetual Imprisonment. The resentment he testified for this made all those tremble that had given the King such Counsel, or that approv'd it. They thought that they should never escape his vengeance, if he recovered one day his Liberty, and they had no rest till they had utterly compleated his ruine.

The Cardinal *Spinosa* remonstrated to the King, That there was a Cage strong enough for this Bird, * and that he would quickly be necessitated, either quite to rid himself of him, or else let him fly.

* *Cathpana* and *Cabrera's* Hist. *Phil* 2 d.

The People, in whose opinion to be justified it is enough to be unfortunate, testified every day more and more their Passion for the Prince being set at Liberty. The King, who was afraid of some Sedition, durst no more absent himself from

H 5   *Madrid*

Madrid; He judged, after a mature deliberation, that there could not be any safety, neither for him nor his Minifters, in fetting the Prince at Liberty; and, that he could no way avoid all that he had reafon to fear from him, but by putting him to death. During fome time, * they mingled in all he took a flow Poyfon, that

* Mr. *de Thou.* le *Laboureur Mayrine*, *Duplex*, &c.

was fpeedily to caufe in him a mortal languifhing; they fpread fome of it upon his wearing Cloathes, upon his Linnen, and generally upon all things that he could touch; but, whether it were that this youth and good conftitution were ftronger then the Poyfon, or that thofe perfons that interefted themfelves in his life, obliged him to make ufe of prefervatives, this way did not fucceed. They muft then explain themfelves more clearly, and the unfortunate Prince was told, * That he might choofe what

* Mat. Hift. of France.

kind

kind of death he pleafed. He received this ftrange news with the indifferency of a man, who loved fomething elfe more then his life, and who feared the fame deftiny for the perfon he loved.

Though the *Spanifh* Hiftorians have fpoken of the weakneffes and paffionate expreffions of this Prince, thereby to blot his memory, and to juftifie his Father; yet it is certain that there never came but one thing out of his Mouth that could pafs for a Complaint; which was, that the Queen having by force of Money found the means of making him be commanded, on her behalf, to ask leave that he might fee the King; as one of his Guards came to him, to tell him, That his Father was coming; *Say my King* (anfwered he) *and not my Father.* * The fubmiffion he had for the Queens Orders, made him refolve to fall upon his knees before the King, and tell him,

* Mr. de *Mezerai* in his great Hift.

him, *That he befeeched him to confider that it was his own blood he was
going to fhed.* The King anfwer'd
him boldly; *That when he had bad
blood, he gave his Arm to the Chirur-
gion to draw it from him.* Don *Carlos* even defperate to have done a
bafenefs without effect, rofe up briskly at thefe words, and askt his Guards
*Whether the Bath in which he was to die
were ready.*

The King, whether it were the
longer to feed his eyes with this barbarous Spectacle, or that perhaps he
was a little fhaken, and fought how
he might handfomly render himfelf,
asked him, *If he had nothing elfe to
fay to him.* The Prince, who would
willingly have redeemed what he had
done at the price of a thoufand other
lives, well perceiving that it was
now too late to husband any thing,
either for him or the Queen, could
not forbear anfwering once for all,
with all his natural fiercenefs; *If
fome perfons* (faid he) *for whom my*
Com-

Complaisance ought not to end but with my life, had not obliged me to see you, I would not have been guilty of the Cowardise of asking you pardon, and I should have dyed more gloriously then you live. The King retir'd himself after this Answer, without shewing any disturbance. Don *Carlos* put himself in the Bath, * and having caused the Veines of his

* *Duplex Eist* of *France*

Armes and Legs to be opened, he commanded all that were present to withdraw. Afterwards taking into his hand a Picture of the Queen in Minitaure, which he alwayes wore about his neck, and which had been the first occasion of his Love, he remained with his eyes fixed upon that fatal Image, till the cold convulsions of death surprized him in that contemplation, and his Soul being already half gone out of his body, with his Blood and Spirits, he lost insensibly his sight, and then his life.

The time of his death is not precisely

cifely known : It is only known, that it arrived a great while before it was publifhed. There was a long Relation of his Sicknefs printed, which they faid was a Malignant Dyfentery, caufed by his diforders.

The Grief of the People, and the defpair of the Princes Domefticks, brake out fo loudly, that the moft paffionate Hiftorians * have not dared to diffemble it. The Count of *Lerma*, whom the King had intrufted with the o-overfight of Don*Carlos*,

* A Relation Printed at *Madrid* in *Spanifh*, and firce at *Venit* in *Italian. Campana Cabrera's* Hift. of *Phil.* 2d, &c.

whilft he was in prifon, had conceived fo extraordinary a Friendfhip for him, that he appeared inconfolable to the eyes of all the Court. The King, to whom thefe regrets were but fo many reproaches, took that way he thought moft certain to make them ceafe; He recompenced magnificently all Don *Carlos* his Servants : He gave the Government of

Cala-

Calatrava to the Count of *Lerma*, and made him Gentleman of his Bed-chamber. It was well seen that these Liberalities were not grounded upon any gratitude for the affection they testified for Don *Carlos*; nevertheless the People diminished nothing of their eagerness to honour this Princes Memory. And it being known that the King designed to make his Obsequies with an extraordinary Magnificence, the Town of *Madrid* demanded, that they might be permitted to be at the Expence of them, and that all the care of performing them, might be left to them. Though the King foresaw that this Funeral would be accompanied with Elegies, which would not be very honourable for the Enemies of the dead Man, he durst not refuse their Petition. *The Historians of his time ＊ *Cabrera's* History of *Philip* the 2d
do particularly extol the tranquility of mind, that he made appear upon the day of that Pomp, when looking

from

from a Window of his Palace upon
the difpofition, and march of the
Ceremony, he decided, upon the place
a difficulty, that was raifed concerning the Precedency of the different
Councils of State that were there
prefent. The two Sons of the Emperour that were then at the Court
of *Spain* were the clofe Mourners.
When they were come near the
Church, * the Cardi-

* *Cabrera's* Hift.
of *Don John*.

nal *Spinofa* who went
before them, imme-
diately after the Body, took leave
of them, and retired himfelf, under
pretence of a pain that took him in
his head. But as he was known for
the moft dangerous, and moft irre-
concileable Enemy Don *Carlos* had
ever had, there were feveral Voices
heard crying round

* *Cabrera's* Hift.
of *Don John*.

about him, * That he
could not fuffer the
prefence of the Prince, neither dead
nor living. The firft thing expofed
to fight, was that famous Encomium

of

of the Scripture for a dead Man, * which was written in great Letters of Gold over the Church-porch. *He hath been ravisht from us, for fear least the Malice of the Age should have chang'd his heart, and least his mind should have been seduced by flattery.* All that an ingenious grief can invent to ease it self, was employed in the proud *Mausoleum*, where this Prince was Interred. But, as all those Ornaments had a reference to the Latin Inscription that served him for an Epitaph, it sufficeth to give the sense of that Inscription, to make the Invention and design of the whole Pomp be comprehended: * *To the eternal Memory of* Charles *Prince of the* Spaines, *of both the* Sicilies, *of the* Gaules, *Belgick and* Cisalpine, *heir of the New World, incomparable in greatness of Soul, in Liberality, and in love for the Truth.* Thus it was that the elevated

*x[>]ν*Wifdome.

* *Relazion de la Muerte y essequias del' prencipe Dem. Carlos.*

vated Genius, and heroical inclinations of the unfortunate Don *Carlos*, were at laſt repreſented under their proper names of Virtues, after having been ſo long diſguiſed by his enemies, under thoſe of Vices.

During the time that the King kept Don *Carlos* his death ſecret, he reſolved to make the news of it be told to the Queen at the time ſhe ſhould be in Travel : He hoped, that ſo ſenſible a trouble of mind, joyned to that of her body, in the condition ſhe was in, would finiſh his revenge ; but he quickly knew, that ſhe was better informed then he deſired. And as ſhe could not be ignorant that Don *Carlos* had been ſacrificed to his Fathers jealouſie,

* *Mr. le Laboureur, upon Caſtelnau, in his Ch. of Don Carlos. Mayerne, &c.*

* ſhe did not at all conſtrain her ſelf to hide the reſentment ſhe had of it. Her juſt anger caſt her Husband into new inquietudes. He thought, he had much to fear from her wit and courage

rage, but yet more from the extraordinary confideration the Court of *France* had for her, and the ftreight correfpondence fhe held with the Queen her Mother.

A few months after the Prince's death, the Dutchefs *d'Alva*, who had one of the chiefeft Offices in the Queen's Houfe, came one morning into her Chamber with a Potion in her hand. The Queen told her, * That fhe was well, and would not take it. But the

* Mr. le Laboureur, Mayerne. M. S. of Mr. Peirefc, &c.

Dutchefs going about to fore her to it, the King, who was not far off, came in at the noife of their conteft: At firft he blamed the Dutchefs for her peremptorinefs; but this woman having reprefented to him, that the Phyficians judged this remedy neceffary for the Queen's happy lying in, he rendred himfelf to their authority. He told the Queen with great fweetnefs, that becaufe this Medicine was of fo great importance,

(156)

tance, she must needs take it. *Because you will have it so* (answered she to him) * *I am contented.* He went immediately out of the Chamber, and some time after came back, * clothed in deep Mourning, to know

* Mr. de *Mezerai*, in his gr. Hist.

* *Mayerne Tar-quett's* History of *Spain.* M. S. of Mr. *Pei-resc, &c.*

how she did. But whether it were, that there was some mistake in the Composition of the Drink, or that the extraordinary disturbance the Queen was in, and the violence she did her self to take it, gave it a malignity which it had not in its self; she expired the same day in the midst of violent pains, and after several great fits of Vomiting. Her Child was found dead, with

* Mr. le Labou-reur.

* its skul almost quite burned away. She was then at the beginning of the four and twentieth year of her age, as well as Don *Carlos*, and in the greatest perfection of her beauty.

For-

Fortune did so exemplarily revenge
the death of these two persons, that
it would be unjust to keep the knowledge of it from posterity. The beauty of the Princess of *Eboli* soon
changed the confidence the King had
in her, into a violent love. *Rui Gomez* her Husband, as jealous of the
confidences the King made to his
Wife, as of the favours she did the
King, resolved to rid himself of her;
but the Princess having discovered
his design, prevented it, by ridding
her self of him. Since that, she kept
Don *John* at a distance from the
Court, under pretence of divers em-
ployments, but in effect, because he
would have treated her with that authority, that their long and familiar
commerce had given him over her;
She made the Government of *Flanders* be given him, in hopes that he
would perish there; as he had done,
if the courage and conduct of the
Prince of *Parma* had not saved him.
In this conjuncture he was told, that
he

he had difcovered the ill offices fhe
had done him. The fear fhe had that
he would ruine her, in letting theKing
know all that had paffed between
them, made her refolve to fhew him
fome Letters of the Prince of *Orange*,
that were of an extraordinary confequence. They imported, that the
Marriage of Don *John* with the
Queen of *England* was concluded,
and that the Rebels of *Flanders* had
engaged their word to acknowledge
him for their Soveraign, as foon as
this marriage fhould be confummated,
and that without any other condition
then Liberty of Confcience. Thefe
Letters were given by *Perez* to the
King, who prefently knew the Prince
of *Orange* his writing; and as he abandon'd himfelf to his fear in the Princefs of *Eholi*'s prefence, fhe took that
time to tell him the anfwer that Don
John had heretofore made to Don
Carlos, when he call'd him Baftard :
She alfo put the King in mind of the
Pride, with which this fame Don
John

John had received the acclamations
of the Army of *Granada*, where the
Souldiers, charmed with some great
action that he had done, cried out in
his presence, *This is the true Son of the
Emperour*, She added his obstinacy to
make himself King of *Tunis*, and the
loss of the *Goulette*, which he had suffer'd to be taken, to revenge himself
upon the King, for not favouring his
designs. These divers reflections,
joyned to the pressing danger of the
pretended Match with *England*, did
penetrate so far into the King's mind,
that thinking he had not the least
time to lose, he found a way of
making a pair of perfum'd walking
Boots be sent to Don *John*, which
cost him his life. Some time after it
was discovered, that the Princess of
Eboli had on purpose made the Prince
of *Orange* write those Letters, which
she said were intercepted, and which
had been so fatal to Don *John*. The
King conceived so great a horrour for
this wickedness, that it extinguish'd
his

his Love. The Princeſs and *Perez* were confin'd to a Priſon, there to end their days. *Perez* afterwards making his eſcape, ſpent the reſt of his life very miſerably, in wandring through all the Princes Courts in *Europe.* And laſt of all, *Philip* the Second himſelf, after he was grown old, among the griefs cauſed him by ſo many diſaſters, was ſtricken with an Ulcer, which bred an incredible quantity of Lice, by which he was even eaten up alive, and ſtifled, when they found no more wherewithall to nouriſh themſelves upon his body. After this manner were expiated the ever to be deplored deaths of a magnanimous Prince, and of the moſt beautiful and moſt virtuous Princeſs that ever was. And thus it was, that their unfortunate Ghoſts were at laſt fully appeaſed, by the Tragical Deſtinies of all the Complices of their Death.

F I N I S.

CPSIA information can be obtained at www.ICGtesting.com
Printed in the USA
LVOW050721060212

267232LV00003B/43/P